Take Your Time
Before Time Takes You

How to Make the Most of Every Day

Copyright © 2025 by Peter Dudley and Gray Bear Publications
All Rights Reserved
No part of this book may be reproduced or retransmitted in any form or by any means, electronic or mechanical, without written permission of the publisher. This book may not be used to train artificial intelligence.

Requests and inquiries may be sent to info@graybearpublications.com. Author is available for speaking, interviews, workshops, and events.

Cover by Peter Dudley
Poetry and photography by Peter Dudley
Published by Gray Bear Publications, an imprint of Gray Bear Coaching, LLC
graybearpublications.com

ISBN: 979-8-9876637-9-0
Also available in paperback and ebook

Dedication

For Cathy and Mark.

Contents

Introduction
Make the Most of Today i

Section 1
Discover Yourself 1
Dear Overachiever: Do Not Skip This Section 3
Your Core Values 7
Your Strengths 23
Limiting Beliefs 31

Section 2
Light the Path 41
Your Future Self is a Demanding Micromanager 43
How You Betray Your Future Self 53
Be Loyal to Yourself 63
Avoid Identity Creep 69
Define Your Fulfilling Life 73
Find Your Own Solutions 79

Section 3
Make It So 83
Life's Not a Sprint. Neither is it a Marathon 85
Someday is Not a Date on the Calendar 89
You're Most Likely to Fail, So What's Stopping You? 95
Stop Planning and Take Action 103
If You Don't Fall Down, You're Not Having Enough Fun 109
What Gets Measured Gets Managed 111
Celebrate Success 117

Section 4
Conclusion 123
Acknowledgements 125
Where to Learn More 126
More from the Author at peterdudley.com 127
About the Author Peter J Dudley, PCC 128

Introduction

Make the Most of Today

September 24, 1987, was not a particularly memorable day. It was my 7,395th day on the planet. I was barely 20 years old. My sister, who was 7 years older and lived on the other side of the country, was enjoying her 10,031st day. It was a Thursday.

Fast forward 26 and a half years, to early summer, 2014.

My sister, now 54 years old, came west for a visit with her two teenage kids. They were about the same ages as my own kids, were nearing high school graduation, and came to California to tour colleges. While they were here, we spent a day walking through Muir Woods surrounded by the giant redwood trees hundreds of years old. Some of those trees sprouted long before the American Revolution. Some sprouted before the Mayflower sailed. And some, perhaps, were even older than the Magna Carta.

My sister was preparing to enjoy an early retirement after a very successful career in finance. I was 47, with a successful and growing career of my own in corporate social impact. As we walked, our conversation turned to the deeper meaning and purpose in life. This often happens when people walk and talk among the redwoods on a quiet day.

"I've spent the first half of my life raising a family," my sister said at one point, "and I've focused entirely on my career and family. Peter, you know a lot about nonprofits, and volunteering, and doing good for the world. I really want to use the second half of my life doing something meaningful for people who need it. Would you help me figure out what that should be?"

"Sure, sis," I answered. "Give me a call when you're ready to talk."

I was eager to have this conversation. The annoying little brother finally getting a chance to guide the bossy big sister! A bonding opportunity after living on opposite coasts our entire adult lives. A topic that would be profoundly and personally meaningful for both of us.

So, when she called me three months later in early September, I answered expecting to have that conversation. I was ready to dig into the causes that inspired her, the kind of legacy she wanted to leave. I had all the questions ready and a set of ideas for her to consider.

Instead of talking about purpose and the second half of her life, however, she told me that she'd just been diagnosed with ALS, and that it was progressing quickly. The following March 12—not even 200 days later—she died. She was 20,062 days old. I was 17,426 days old.

September 24, 1987, was not a particularly memorable day. It would have been, however, had we known at the time that it was the exact halfway point of my sister's life. She lived 10,031 days up to that point. She lived another 10,031 days after that point.

I will never forget the phrase she used walking in the forest that summer day in 2014: "The second half of my life." Under the redwoods, neither of us had any idea that the second half of her life had begun 26 years earlier and was already coming to an end.

I wonder what date marked the halfway point of my life. At 57 years old as I write this, I'm pretty sure it's already passed. Perhaps not, but very likely.

What date will mark the midpoint of your life, do you think? That day when your life is half gone? The date after which you have fewer days left than days you've lived? If you knew what that date was, would it change how you approach today? Would it change how you think about family, relationships, work, wealth, health?

That phone call with my sister absolutely changed the way I thought about my life. It changed the way I thought about today, tomorrow, and next week. It changed the way I thought about the coming decades and what I wanted to do with them… if I was fortunate enough to have them.

Time became suddenly very precious, and I vowed to myself that from that moment forward, I would make the most of every day. What "the most" might mean was breathtakingly unclear, of course. What does it mean to make the most of today? What does it mean to make the most of this month? This year?

How does someone even go about answering that question? The one thing that was clear to me at that moment was that no two people I asked would be likely to give the same answer. I knew nonprofit leaders who would have told me to focus on serving others and making the world a better place. I knew a few high achievers who would have told me that "make the most of today" would mean never wasting a single second of productive time. I had friends who would have advised that "family is everything," whatever that means. And others who would have told me to "follow my passions."

But at that moment, approaching 50 years old, I had no idea how much time I had to plan for, or what any given day would bring. I was unclear on what "make the most of every day" meant, but I was extremely clear on two things:

1. I was not going to waste any time or energy judging myself for getting it wrong, and
2. I did not want to waste any time or energy worrying about what other people thought about my choices.

Both were easier promised than accomplished, I can assure you.

It would be six more years before I got into professional coaching. During those six years, I made it my personal mission to find my way to a fulfilling, complete life with both peace and purpose. At first, it was haphazard and clumsy. I stepped on some toes and burned a few bridges I now wish I hadn't. Other bridges, however, I do not regret burning at all, and I am glad to leave in my past.

As I learned more about myself, my core values, and what I truly wanted in life, my efforts became more intentional and directed. I've made lots of mistakes along the way, and I hope to make many more.

This book, however, is not about me. It's about you.

Introduction: Make the Most of Today | v

If you've come to this book looking for answers, I'm going to give you permission to hand it off to someone else right now.

If you're looking for answers, you can find tons of people eager to take your money in return for a few bits of fridge magnet wisdom. I believe that these people are, by and large, not charlatans. They believe what they're selling. The problem is, if someone promises they have the answers to life's confusing and complicated messiness, they're almost always selling something that fits them uniquely well, but which probably won't fit you very well.

There is no reliably repeatable recipe for a fulfilling life. That's because we're all working with a different set of ingredients and a different set of tools, under a different set of conditions. And we all have our own unique vision for what the term "fulfilling life" means.

In the same way we each must decide for ourselves what "make the most of today" means, we also each must decide for ourselves what "fulfilling" looks like. So, even though I have a lot of answers, I'm not selling answers because I don't have *your* answers. I have *my* answers. What I do have for you, however, is all the questions I learned to ask along the way to get to my answers. I have the perspective-twisting and mind-opening exercises and observations that challenged me to think differently, that shined a bright light on my limiting beliefs, and that helped me find my own path to fulfillment.

These questions, observations, and exercises are tools that I continue to use today and expect to use throughout the rest of my life because "fulfillment" is not a destination. It's a state of being. It's a way of living. It's how I remind myself to make the most of every day.

September 24, 1987 was not a particularly memorable day. My walk through the woods with my sister 26 years later, however, was a very memorable day, as was the day she called to let me know she was not going to get the second half of her life she had been expecting.

That conversation I never had with my sister, I think, is what led me to the vocation of professional coaching. The conversation that didn't happen… that is my unfinished business. I can't have that conversation with her, but I can have it with you. I can't help her figure out what a meaningful, fulfilling second half to life would look like for her, but I can help you.

And that's the reason for this book.

Miss you, sis.

Section 1

Discover Yourself

This section focuses on who you are as an individual at this point in your life. We'll get into who you want to become and how to get there in later chapters, but first it's important to know where you're starting. In this section you'll learn how to

- Identify your core values, why they're important, and how they can guide you,
- Identify your strengths and understand what it means to be strengths-oriented, and
- Begin understanding when limiting beliefs might be holding you back.

Write down your goals and hopes for reading this book. What do you want to be different from having read it and gone through all the exercises? What have you not yet accomplished that you wish to?

Dear Overachiever: Do Not Skip This Section

You're probably eager to move forward and get to work on reaching your goals. After all, it's that kind of can-do, action-oriented attitude that's brought you success all your life, right? Let's go!

If that's the case, now is the most important time to pause, take a few deep breaths, and break out of that mode. If you're reading this book (and you are, obviously), then you are here because you want change, in some form.

"But I already know who I am," you may think. "I'm very self-aware." In my experience, the people who think they know themselves are some of the least self-aware people there are. Highly Successful people tend to believe that their success comes from who they are, not what they've done, and thus they conflate outcomes with identity. But I'm getting ahead of myself.

It's possible you'll get to the end of this chapter and feel profoundly validated. If so, you can probably skip the rest of this book. You already know who you are, what you need to do, and how to do it. So just get off your ass and do it already. There you go. You're welcome. I just saved you several hours of reading, introspection, thought, and growth.

It's far more likely, and indeed it is my goal, that if you approach this section with honesty, intention, and patience, you will have at least one (and perhaps several) perspective-altering insights about yourself. And that, my friend, is where growth and change begin. Growth and change require more than just motion. The most furious, energetic, and inspired motion can keep sending you in circles, right back to where you are right now.

You've got to know where you're starting, where you want to go, and the difference between those two things before you start moving. Otherwise, you'll probably end up making fragile promises to yourself about superficial change that won't actually affect how you feel about your life. Then, a year from now, you might wonder why this book didn't actually help you change your life. Just like all the other books you've tried that didn't change your life.

So if you're still reading (and you are, obviously), then that means you're ready to make real, lasting, and meaningful change.

What to Expect

The process of self-improvement is incredibly simple. It's about knowing yourself, knowing what you want to be, and doing the things that will get you to that point. That's it. There's no magic to it. Know yourself. Know what you want to be. Do the things that get you there.

It's all about you. It's not about the methodology in the book or the knowledge and wisdom of your coach. It's about you, your self-awareness, your clarity, and your capability.

The tools, exercises, approaches, and stories in this book are meant to help you with self-awareness and clarity. Most of them seem simple on the surface, but allow yourself the time you'll need to complete each one honestly and thoroughly. Transformation can sometimes be a switch-flip experience, where you gain a profound insight that changes everything. It can take a lot of work and a long time to find the right switch to flip, however.

The exercises are meant to help you understand your capability, to identify the actions you need to take, and to feel confident that those actions will get you the change you need.

You'll still need to take those actions. So if you've been working on life change—bouncing from one methodology to the next without the results you're hoping for—it's time to understand that the magic isn't in a methodology, a coach, or a retreat. The magic is in you. (Yes, I said it, and I hate myself a little bit for it.)

Here are a few journal prompts to use after completing each chapter:

- *List a few key ideas from the chapter that you want to take with you through the rest of the book.*
- *How will you return to these key ideas and keep putting them to use in the future?*
- *Write down the insights you gained about yourself by doing the chapter's exercises.*
- *What two or three things do you want to focus on in the coming week based on the learnings you just gained? These might include things like new approaches to an existing problem, or a different way of communicating, or letting go of a limiting belief... whatever you are inspired to work on, whether it is related directly to the chapter's content or not.*
- *Read and reflect on a journal entry you wrote after one of the previous chapters. How are you doing on those changes you intended to make at that time? How will you continue (or revive) that effort in the coming week?*
- *Who can you enlist as an ally in helping you follow through on these intentions?*

Your Core Values

Most people don't think too deeply about their core values. We go through life *thinking* we know what's important to us, but a lot of that is determined for us by external factors. Those things may be part of your larger value system, but who are you, *really*, at your core?

When you're living a life that aligns with your core values, you feel in sync with things. But when you're living a life that is in conflict with one or more of your core values, you may feel out of place, like you're wearing sweatpants at a fancy dinner, or a tuxedo at a barbecue. People use words like "stuck" or "unmotivated" or "lost" when they're living a life that feels not quite right. They say things like, "I don't know what I want, but I know I don't want *this*."

Your value system drives the decisions you make every day. Small decisions such as which loaf of bread to buy at the grocery store. Big decisions such as whether to ask for a divorce.

All the inputs coming at us for each of these decisions get filtered through our own personal value system. The complexity and volume of information coming in at every moment can make even the simplest of decisions feel complicated.

Which loaf of bread to buy turns out to have a lot of variables. Price, nutrition, packaging, flavor, how much time you have, aesthetic, and even who happens to be standing next to you at that moment. It might even be a frustrating and difficult choice because your kids like the bread that is less nutritious, and you'd feel less shame at checkout when the clerk sees you picked the environmentally friendly brand. At some point, all these conflicting values either sort themselves out and you pick a loaf of bread to buy, or you wander off in despair, humiliation, and shame.

That may seem a trivial example, but I'm guessing you felt some feelings while reading it. Maybe it's not about bread, but I would bet good money that you've felt that kind of conflict of values in a number of small decisions.

We make all these decisions through our own personal value system. If we don't understand our core values, the values being inflicted upon us by others, and the difference between them, then we may end up making the same bad decisions over and over and over again. Or even if they're not bad decisions per se, they may be wrong decisions that lead to us getting off track or ending up right back where we started.

How, then, do you figure out what your core values are? It's a very simple exercise, but it takes deep introspection and honest self-assessment. These are things a lot of very successful people don't have much practice with. The following exercises will help you identify your own core values and how they intersect or conflict with the external value systems influencing you.

Write Down Your Unwritten Rules

Unwritten rules are often at the core of any interpersonal conflict—in the workplace, in families, and in communities.

At one of my jobs, the department head brought in a consultant after a big merger to run a workshop with our whole group of about 100 employees. At one point in her presentation, this consultant asked the group, "What are the unwritten rules of this workplace?"

The question hit most of us sideways. Unwritten rules? This was a Big Bank. Every rule was written down. In fact, it often seemed there were far too many written-down rules to remember half of them. Nah, there weren't any unwritten rules. Were there?

It didn't take long, however, for people to start calling out aspects of the company's culture that weren't written down anywhere. Even the simplest things like "meetings start on time" and "you always answer the phone when the boss calls" started to open our eyes. Most of us had never thought about the unwritten rules that governed our workplace.

Every culture has unwritten rules. When those rules feel comfortable to you, you don't even notice them. But when you're out of sync with them, they can really throw you off. Imagine coming from a workplace where every decision requires a meeting, then going into a workplace where people don't even schedule meetings—they just pop into your office whenever they have something to talk about. You'd think they were all utterly mad, wildly insensitive sociopaths. Imagine marrying into a rigidly patriarchal family when you grew up in a flexible, egalitarian family. Imagine moving from a heavily micromanaged environment into a space of empowering creative ownership. Disorienting!

Every one of these cultures has its own set of unwritten rules, and once you internalize that ruleset, it can be hard to understand how it drives your own behavior. When not everyone is working with the same set of unwritten rules, or not everyone has the same understanding of those rules, it can lead to dysfunction. Worse, it can become almost impossible to diagnose that dysfunction because everyone begins to think that everyone else is the problem.

When you're unaware of your own role in a dysfunctional situation, you tend to blame everyone and everything else for all the problems. While I have not met every human who ever existed, and I don't have scientifically generated data to extrapolate from, I feel confident in saying that this is a pretty universal human behavior.

One of the few memorable lessons I took from my training as a boy scout leader was this: "The boys you're leading really only want two things: They want to know what the rules are, and they want to know that the rules will be enforced." This is also generally true with grownups. We all want to know what the rules are, and we all want to know that the rules will be applied the same way for all people.

Ambiguous or inconsistently enforced rules cause confusion and discord. Clear rules make maintaining order and courtesy a straightforward matter of education and enforcement. Everyone can at least agree what the system *is*, whether or not they agree that it should be that way. But unwritten rules aren't officially the same for all people, so we each import our own version of them. We each bring our own ideas of how people are supposed to act and interact.

When other people break your unwritten rules, you don't blame yourself for having incorrect rules. You blame the other people for their incorrect behavior. And, very likely, they are simultaneously blaming you for your incorrect behavior.

Write down your own unwritten rules. Don't worry if you aren't sure how to do this. Don't expect to get them all on the first pass. At this point, the intention is to start becoming aware of the ways that you think, that might be different from how others from different backgrounds or different mindsets think.

There is no right or wrong, no good or bad here. As you'll find throughout these exercises, simply observing as objectively as possible, without judgment, is the goal.

Here are a few of my own unwritten rules, for example:

- Be on time.
- If you take the last of the coffee, make a new pot.
- Freaking out is not a path to creative solutions.
- No hitting. No insults. No cruelty.
- There are always more than two options in every choice.
- Everyone has freedom of choice, but no one has freedom from consequence.
- Calendars exist so I don't have to remember every appointment.
- Emotions are real and should be recognized and felt.
- Interrupting or talking over other people is rude.

Those are just a few of the many unwritten rules (I guess now they *are* written) that guide my day-to-day. Many are expectations I carry about human behavior that come from my upbringing, or that I've developed over the course of my 57 years.

Some of them still cause tension, conflict, and discord even today, like the last one: "Interrupting or talking over other people is rude." In my mind, it's simply common courtesy to let whoever is speaking finish their thought before adding your own.

Not everyone thinks that way. I get into a room with a family of over-talkers, and it feels like I've been dropped into a pit filled with geese that have been fed cocaine. I stand there with things I'd like to add to the conversation, but there always seem to be at least two voices talking in every moment, and by the time there's even a narrow opening, the conversation has changed topics three or four times and the thing I wanted to say has become irrelevant.

My unwritten rules of conversation, which are deeply ingrained from earliest childhood, tell me that the over-talker family's behavior is rude and selfish. But their unwritten rules of conversation are the exact opposite of mine. To them, good conversationalists are active speakers, adding their spirited, vigorous participation whenever they have a relevant thought, no matter how many other voices are filling the space. To them, I'm the odd one. They probably think me rude and aloof, or slow and introverted.

This is a real thing that has happened to me on more than one occasion, and not just in social situations. It happens in the workplace, too. Imagine when three people who grew up in over-talker families are in a meeting with three people from families like mine. The over-talkers end up using all the air in the room, leaving no space for the others who feel left farther and farther behind. The quieter, more structure-oriented participants get mislabeled as introverted, or, worse, underperformers.

All because the unwritten rules they each bring with them into the meeting aren't aligned.

Write down as many of your own unwritten rules as you can. Here are some questions to help you get started and to pique your imagination:

1. What bothers me about others' behavior in a crowded restaurant?
2. How do I typically react to unexpected changes in plans?
3. What are my thoughts on personal space and physical touch?
4. What topics of conversation are inappropriate at a business event?
5. How do I express gratitude and appreciation?
6. How do I expect others to express gratitude and appreciation?
7. How do I typically behave at a casual dinner party where I only know some of the people?
8. How do I expect my romantic partner to behave when I am sad?
9. What do I expect from a friend who disagrees with me?
10. How involved should parents be in their children's school?
11. What does loyalty mean to me, and how should people express it?

Define Your Core Values

To define your core values, you not only have to understand what you care about, but you also have to become keenly aware of the influence others have on what you think you care about. This is the difference between what's truly important to you, and what others tell you should be important to you. While these two sets probably overlap, that overlap may be less than you expect.

Why is this important? Consider a camel.

> *"A camel is a horse designed by committee."*
> *- Reportedly Alec Issigonis*

Camels are remarkably well adapted to the desert environment. Their nostrils recapture exhaled moisture. Their mouths have a thick, leathery lining so they can eat prickly desert vegetation. Camels are also odd-looking creatures with goofy long necks, strange humps, ungainly gait, and shaggy faces. They have a reputation for being cranky and cantankerous, and for spitting when they're upset.

Horses and camels share some characteristics. Both have four longish legs. Both can be ridden by humans and used to carry heavy burdens. Both eat plants and drink water. Both have tails. They have differences, too, and it's fair to say that a camel is very good at being a camel, but it is not very good at being a horse.

Imagine you want a creature designed for you. You write up a spec sheet, then hire a committee to design and build that creature. The creature you imagine looks and behaves very much like a horse. Your specifications say the creature

Your Core Values | 15

This is neither a camel nor a horse.

- Must live on land, eat readily available vegetation, and hydrate with water
- Must be able to move quickly across diverse terrain
- Must be able to carry heavy loads and pull a wheeled cart
- Must be able to carry a human rider long distances

You deliver the spec sheet to your committee, trusting that they will deliver you the exact creature to meet your needs. What you don't realize is how the biases, experiences, and beliefs of each committee member will influence the design. One lives with their large family in a desert. One is a cartoonist whose dysfunctional romantic relationships always end in drama. One is a grumpy, reclusive curmudgeon. One is a Wall Street executive. Who knows what they might come up with? It might be a camel. It might be a mountain goat. It might be a triceratops. It's possible—but unlikely—that they design exactly what you need, which in this case is a horse.

Now imagine you're facing a big life decision. Should you quit this job? Should you move across the country to care for your aging mother? Should you try out for America's Got Talent? Should you fire that difficult employee? Is now the time to start that home business?

You have a hard time deciding, so you approach several people who care about you and whom you know and trust. You're certain that they all want the best for you, and you think they're all smart and wise. You know they all understand that you

- Want to be happy
- Want to be secure
- Want to be valued
- Want to be healthy

You ask for their advice, trusting that they will make the best decision for you. What you don't realize is how the biases, experiences, and beliefs of each committee member will influence their opinions. One lives with their large family in a desert. One is a cartoonist whose dysfunctional romantic relationships always end in drama. One is a grumpy, reclusive curmudgeon. One is a Wall Street executive.

They each know what would make *them* feel happy, secure, valued, and healthy. How likely is it that they will know what will make *you* feel happy, secure, valued, and healthy? It's possible they might get lucky with some advice that fits, but more likely the advice they give you—the life they design for you—will match what *they* want, not what *you* need.

That is how externally imposed values end up driving you to bad decisions.

I'm not against asking people what they think, and I'm not against taking someone else's advice. There is a huge difference, however, between asking advice from smart people, and allowing others to make your decisions for you. There's also a huge difference between knowing what's important to you and allowing others to decide what should be important to you.

The problem with handing over your power to others—whether directly or through the implicit value systems of family, culture, faith, etc.—is that you always get what would be right for those others. If you're very, very lucky, it might also be right for you, too. More often than not, however, you get good advice that feels like it doesn't quite fit. When you live your life following good advice that doesn't quite fit, you're going to live with a constant, vague sense that something is wrong. And because you can't identify what's wrong—you took everyone's advice, after all—then you start to feel the shame and guilt of feeling unhappy or discontented even when everything *seems* to be going right.

You wanted a horse, but everyone said you should have a camel, so you got a camel. It does everything you wanted your creature to do, and everyone says it's a lovely creature. But it is not, and it never will be, a horse. So, you can either find a way to be happy with a camel, or you can own your authenticity, find your agency, and make the change you need.

This became clear to me early on in my career, when a friend was telling me about his father. This man had been bitter and angry about his work for years. He blamed work obligations for taking all his time, making him miss his kids' events, running him ragged with travel. Then one day, he realized he could choose. He could choose a different job. He could refuse to travel so much. He could demand not to be worked so hard. Each of those choices would have different consequences, but until that moment, he had never realized these choices were available to him.

He chose to keep living in just the same way as he had been, but because he finally realized that it was his choice and that he was making that decision intentionally and on his own terms, he stopped blaming others and was no longer bitter and resentful. He decided that the camel was, in fact, what he really needed.

He had been in conflict. He had felt trapped. You might think he felt trapped in a bad, demanding job. The truth was, he was trapped between two sets of competing external value systems: On the one hand, his boss and society told him he needed to make money, be successful, and advance his career. On the other hand, his family, friends, and society told him he needed to spend time with family, value balance, and live a well-rounded life. This is a position many of us have felt stuck in. You may even be feeling it right now.

My friend's father suffered with bitter resentment for decades. He didn't see a way out that would make everyone else happy. Ultimately, he connected to his own core values and realized he could choose the way of life that would make *him* happy.

Ask people what's important to them, and mostly they'll say something like, "Obviously family, happiness, and helping others." All the things we are *supposed* to hold dear.

But what are your true core values? When you strip away all the shoulds in your life, when you cast off the externally imposed value systems of your family, social groups, faith groups, society… what do you truly care about most? Only once you've articulated that can you see where you align with or depart from the other value systems influencing your life. Only then can you be intentional and deliberate about the choices you make in being authentic versus fitting in.

A Worksheet to Define Your Core Values

Look at the list on the next page. Circle all the words that resonate with you as your personal values. If a word comes to you that's not on this list, add it!

Take your time and consider if these are truly *your* values or if they are values that society or other people tell you *should* be important to you.

To narrow it down, ask yourself:

- How do these values define me?
- Is this who I am at my best?
- How do my actions reflect these values?
- Are these values a filter I use to make hard decisions?

Accountability	Fairness	Motivation
Achievement	Family	Nature
Adventure	Focus	Open Mindedness
Ambition	Freedom	Persistence
Appearance	Fulfillment	Relationships
Approval	Fun	Reputation
Authenticity	Growth	Respect
Authority	Happiness	Responsibility
Awareness	Hard Work	Risk-Taking
Balance	Health	Security
Belonging	Helping Others	Self-Development
Career	Honesty	Self-Expression
Children	Humility	Self-Respect
Collaboration	Humor	Social Recognition
Conformity	Improving Society	Spirituality
Contribution	Individualism	Status
Creativity	Inner Peace	Success
Culture	Integrity	Superiority
Curiosity	Intelligence	Talent
Education	Joy	Teaching
Effectiveness	Kindness	Teamwork
Energy	Leadership	Tolerance
Environment	Learning	Tranquility
Equality	Love	Trust
Excellence	Loyalty	Truthfulness
Expertise	Modesty	Wealth

After circling all the words that resonate most with you, write down the ten most important in the blank spaces below. These should be the ten that are most important to *you* in how you live your life.

1. _____   2. _____

3. _____   4. _____

5. _____   6. _____

7. _____   8. _____

9. _____   10. _____

Now, cross out five of those ten words, keeping only the five most important. Take your time to think through each of these. It can be very difficult to drop words from your list at this point because you've already said these are all important to you. Think about tough situations when you might be forced to choose between two of these important values. Which one feels more "right" when conflicting with the others? Which do you honor the most in difficult decisions?

Now that you've cut it down to five core values, pick the three most important and write them in the lines on the next page. If you can only get down to four, try harder. The whole point of this exercise is for you to think deeply about those values you hold deeper than any others, the values at the core of your identity and upon which you wish to live your life.

My Top Three Core Values

_____

_____

_____

This is not to say that the other values you left behind are meaningless! You are a whole person, after all, with rich complexity and a variety of interests, cares, worries, and influences. These three core values provide a kind of north star that can help you avoid identity creep when making decisions where your values conflict. (You'll learn more about identity creep later in this book.)

These, also, are neither camels nor horses.

Your Strengths

I learned quite by accident that to live a more fulfilling life and be happier and more successful in my career, I needed to focus on things I was good at and stop trying to be good at the things that were difficult. When you're in a position to rely on your strengths instead of struggle with your weaknesses, you have an easier time achieving goals, completing tasks, and working with others. This is called a strengths-based approach to life and work.

The second key to a strengths-based approach is the willingness to allow yourself to be bad at some things. In our achievement-oriented culture, we are obsessed with filling in our perceived gaps. "I need to get better at X" is far too common a phrase. While being good at lots of things is beneficial, being too focused on improving your weaknesses is a sure way to make a daily practice of struggle and frustration.

Imagine you're driving somewhere, on a two-lane highway. One of the two lanes is littered with debris and pocked with potholes the entire way. The other is clear, smooth, and recently paved. If you're in a constant mode of "I need to get better at driving through debris and avoiding potholes," you will take the cruddy lane and struggle through the rough ride, ultimately getting to your destination late, exhausted, and frustrated, and possibly with a beat-up car.

If, however, you drive in the clear lane, you can get to your destination happy, energized, and ready to move on to whatever's next. That's what it feels like when you're able to rely on your natural talents and strengths in your day-to-day life.

I learned this idea somewhat by accident around the time I turned 30, when I was head of marketing for a small tech startup. I and my two-person team did a tremendous amount of work—we rebranded the company and product line, designed brochures, published articles, built a website, ran seminars and trade shows, supported the sales team, etc.

Every day, however, I went home feeling guilty. Each day I had 50 things to do and time to do only 40 of them. It's not unusual to have more work than you can do—if you don't, you may not have a big enough vision. But something nagged at me, something that was bigger than "not enough time." Some of the tasks seemed to keep falling farther and farther behind.

Humans are terrible self-reporters. Without data, we make decisions based on feelings, and our feelings are terribly polluted with all kinds of biases and misinformation. So I decided to track my own performance and see whether my feelings—that I was not doing very well at my job—were accurate.

I started with a daily habit I was already doing: my daily to-do list. My habit was such that each morning, I'd take yesterday's to-do list and copy the undone tasks to a new page. I'd then add anything that was new for today and throw away yesterday's list. For my new effort, I simply began putting yesterday's to-do list in my desk drawer instead of the trash. After three months, I pulled out all those lists and looked them over. This exercise taught me two things:

First, that I had accomplished a hell of a lot more than I was giving myself credit for. The number and scope of the items I crossed off each day reassured me I was, in fact, killing it.

Second, that there was a very clear pattern in the items that were left undone at the end of each day. Day after day, the same types of tasks were the ones that fell to the bottom of the list. It wasn't because they were less urgent or important; everything on my list was urgent and important. It was because of the type of work they required. I learned that when having to choose between two tasks, I tended to do the ones that I was naturally good at and leave the others for later, even if those others were smaller and simpler.

When I realized that, I decided I should never take a job where those kinds of tasks were critical to my own success. I wouldn't know until many years later that what I'd just done was take a strengths-based approach to my work. I decided that I should put myself in a position to spend most of my effort doing the things I am naturally good at, since that was what I was doing anyway.

While all my jobs since that day have in fact required the doing of many things I am not naturally good at, I have learned to fill those gaps in other ways. This has not only kept me from being exhausted and worn down by doing things I struggle with, but it has amplified my own effectiveness by allowing me to do more of the things I'm good at.

Assess Your Strengths

There are several good strengths assessments on the market that I recommend to my clients. If you are really interested in going deep on your strengths, I recommend picking one and paying for their report. They give you a thorough starting point for a conversation with yourself, and a shared language if you're in a conversation with others (e.g., a workgroup). I even offer an assessment on my own website at graybearcoaching.com (look for the Life Purpose Assessment).

You don't need a branded commercial assessment, however, to identify your own strengths. You can simply reflect as objectively as possible on your own work and tendencies, as I did. It helps to get feedback from others as well.

Perhaps the simplest way to do this is to look at a list of common strengths and grade yourself on them.

Consider the 51 strengths listed in the table on page 28. For each, write a number from 1 to 10 beside the word. A 1 represents that this is a strength you are not good at, that brings up feelings of discomfort, and which you do not rely on in your daily life or for important things. A 10 is a strength that feels easy to you, something that helps you get things done and which feels comfortable.

This is not as easy as it sounds. We often admire the strengths that other people have while failing to recognize our own. This exercise is not about picking the strengths you admire or wish you had. It's about building self-awareness by reflecting on how you've achieved your own successes and the unique value you bring to any situation. That is, don't give high scores to the words that represent things you admire in other people, or which you would strive to improve. Give high scores to the ones you can point to as helping in your successes to date. For example, if you *value* compassion but you are the one who always brings clarity, fairness, and integrity to every situation while others play the bleeding heart, then perhaps you should not give compassion a high score.

Then, go back through and highlight the ones that you graded seven or higher. Look at the mix of words you chose. Reflect on the diversity of those words and the commonalities between them. What do you think this tells you about yourself? What types of activities do they point you toward? What else can you learn about yourself? Share your self-assessment with trusted people who know you, and ask what they think. If they disagree with any of your assessment, this should make you curious, not upset. Accept their answers as a truth that you had not yet been aware of, rather than a thing to be argued away. Think of the times in your life that serve as evidence for what they're saying, and the times that serve as evidence against what they're saying.

Adaptability	Fairness	Learning Agility
Analytical Thinking	Flexibility	Listening
Authenticity	Focus	Love of Learning
Bravery	Forgiveness	Open-Mindedness
Catalyzing Change	Generosity	Optimism
Clarity	Gratitude	Organization
Compassion	Grit	Patience
Confidence	Honesty	Perseverance
Connection	Humility	Practicality
Creativity	Humor	Problem-Solving
Curiosity	Influence	Resilience
Decision-Making	Initiative	Resourcefulness
Determination	Innovation	Self-Control
Discernment	Integrity	Strategic Thinking
Discipline	Intuition	Teamwork
Empathy	Kindness	Vision
Enthusiasm	Leadership	Work Ethic

Reflect on Your Experiences

Describe a situation where success seemed to come easily. How did that feel? What strengths helped you get it done?

Describe a situation where you succeeded, but getting it done was a real struggle. How did that feel? What skills did you struggle with, or what gaps in your strengths can you identify from that time?

How do your strenghts show up when you are successful?

Limiting Beliefs

Limiting beliefs hold people back. Your own self-limiting beliefs or others' limiting beliefs about you may be creating fake obstacles that seem insurmountable. Your limiting beliefs about others may be destroying relationships.

Limiting beliefs are perhaps the most insidious of all human traits because they become self-fulfilling. When people have a belief, our confirmation bias guides us to see evidence of that belief while ignoring evidence that refutes that belief. Over time, that belief becomes more and more entrenched, and we even begin to *create* evidence that supports the false belief.

Sometimes it's easy to know where a limiting belief originated, as in the case of a doctor I once worked with. She had been told (wrongly) by her high school English teacher that she was a terrible writer. She spent her entire adult life believing it and avoiding situations where she might have to write. When an opportunity came up to contribute her professional expertise by writing a chapter for a book, she was terrified and almost turned it down. I told her I'd help her get through it, but as it turns out she needed very little help. She was a natural storyteller, had strong command of language, and was very efficient with her words.

I have mixed feelings about the teacher that told her she was a bad writer because on the one hand, they created the limiting belief with a judgmental remark during a formative period in a young person's life. On the other hand, who knows how my client's life may have been different without that belief about herself? I can't say with certainty that the teacher's remark didn't cause her to keep working to hone skills under the belief that she would never be good enough. Regardless, having identified this limiting belief, she now has a different perspective on her writing skill and more confidence to finally begin writing the things she has wanted to work on for many years.

Often, it's nearly impossible to understand where the limiting belief originated. Unpacking the baggage someone is carrying is one of the things professional therapy is for; if you discover you have limiting beliefs you were unaware of before and have trouble overcoming them, you may want to work with a licensed therapist on getting to the root of that belief. That kind of deep emotional excavation can lead to profound learning about yourself, which you can then begin to work on in productive ways.

In my case, I was made aware of one of my own self-limiting beliefs when a colleague laughed at me in front of my whole team. I was 44 years old and had recently been promoted to an executive role in a big company, managing a team of seven people running some very large, very visible programs. One of the first things I did as manager was to bring my whole team together for an offsite planning meeting. In addition to the project work that I'd put on our agenda, I wanted to build team camaraderie and rapport, so I brought in a facilitator to help the team do a group strengths exercise. During the discussion, the facilitator asked if any of us had been surprised by the results of the strengths assessment.

I spoke up immediately. My assessment had come back with a number of relationship-oriented strengths among my top themes. This couldn't have been right because I was shy and reserved. I had always considered myself an introvert. I was not one to be aggressive or take over meetings. In fact, one of my previous managers had once told me that I needed to speak up more because I had a lot of good ideas and thoughts that went unheard. I still remember him saying, "Still waters run deep" when trying to encourage me to speak up more.

As soon as I told the facilitator that I was not a social, relationship-oriented person, one of my team members laughed out loud. This was not a mild chortle or knowing snicker. It was a great bark of a laugh. A guffaw that would shake the chandeliers, if there had been chandeliers in this windowless conference room.

When she stopped laughing, she said, "Oh come on, Peter. I've watched you work a room."

This startled and disoriented me. I was shy, wasn't I? I was reserved, wasn't I? I was quiet and restrained. Right?

Wrong.

When I look back at my life as objectively as possible, I see that I had some shyness as a kid, but I also had a lot of friends. Somewhere along the line, perhaps in my early 20s, I began to believe I was introverted and reserved. I can't really say when that happened or how, and when the strengths assessment came back with all the relationship-oriented strengths floating to the top, I was surprised.

"Oh come on, Peter. I've watched you work a room."

I had expected my strengths assessment would highlight other areas. When it didn't, I had a choice: I could reject the report and call the whole thing flawed, or I could accept this new piece of data and examine it with curiosity. I chose the latter, and that opened my mind to reexamine my actual behaviors in a new light.

I spent a lot of time over the next few months journaling and thinking back over my life. What evidence supported this new data? What eveidence refuted it?

As a kid, I was always in the thick of things, often planning or instigating social activities. In high school, I rarely spent afternoons or weekends at home, instead spending time with one of my many friend groups. In hindsight, I now marvel at how many different friend groups I was part of and how many activities I managed to participate in as a teenager.

Later, in college, I made friends relatively easily. I had always attributed that to other people being the ones who started new conversations, but looking back with a different lens, I began to see how my behavior encouraged those conversations, and how I put myself in positions where social connections could take root. I wouldn't say I was a "joiner" or notably extroverted, but I definitely was not introverted or overly shy.

This continued into my early career, when I often found myself in situations that pushed the limits of my comfort zone. I had attributed a lot of that to luck, to privilege, and to being in the right place at the right time. Looking back with a different lens, I can see that although luck, privilege, and timing all played a role, some of that was made possible by how I showed up in the world: friendly, affable, open, interested, curious… the things that correlate to relationship-oriented strengths.

"Oh come on, Peter. I've watched you work a room."

What my colleague was referring to, I realized, was the many work conferences and events she and I had attended together. Over the years, I had indeed built up a substantial network, and as I thought back over how I'd done that, it became clear that I did, indeed, work a room. Not in a cynical, mercenary, smarmy kind of way, but in a legitimate "oh look there is a person, I bet they are interesting" kind of way.

I thought a lot about this new data point and the new perspective it gave me over the next several months. As I journaled about it, I observed my current behaviors as objectively as possible, without judgment. As a result of all this reflection, I realized that the strengths assessment had been correct. And, perhaps, I should in fact begin honoring and developing those talents instead of ignoring and even suppressing them.

The lesson I'm sharing is not about introvert versus extrovert, but about how we can take small misconceptions and turn them into limiting beliefs, how those limiting beliefs can gain a life of their own until they become unquestioned truths, and how new externally generated data can prompt a reexamination of those beliefs that may lead to much deeper self-awareness. I unlocked a part of me that I'd shut away because somehow, I had come to falsely believe that's not who I really was. Very like the doctor who shut off her writing for much of her life because one authority figure told her to, even though she was in fact a very good writer.

There's a legitimate question to be asked at this point, however: Did my strengths assessment reflect a truth about me I didn't previously know, or did I adjust my behavior on the power of its suggestion? Did I swap one type of limiting belief (I am an introvert) for another (I am relationship-oriented), and was my confirmation bias leading me to seek and find new evidence to support that new belief? Certainly, that was possible, and it's one of the things you have to be careful about when giving power to any assessment tool or external opinion. All those tools should be treated with some amount of healthy skepticism and critical analysis.

That's why I not only tried to view my own behavior as objectively as I could, but I also sought out the opinions of other people I trusted who knew me well. The more distance I got from my original limiting belief, the less I believed it. And the less I believed it, the more I was able to see opportunity for myself in situations that before had seemed like opportunity for others.

That made a huge difference in my career over the next decade. I took on more leadership roles with industry councils and conferences, I was more intentional and courageous about building my professional network, I picked up my volunteering with youth sports and scout leadership, and—most important—I trusted myself more in all those situations.

I didn't suddenly become the party planner or the guy who leapt out onto center stage at every event. I don't sing karaoke or do improv. Those kinds of activities still mostly terrify me. Stepping up to an open mic to read my poetry still sends my heart racing, even when I know the audience is friendly and supportive.

Instead, I learned how to view my strengths outside the preconceived notions of what a social and relationship-oriented person looks like. By expanding my limited definition of those terms, I was able to see more space where I could fit. That opened up the idea of opportunity where I had always seen barriers and closed doors. And that is the power you find when you understand and begin to dismantle your own limiting beliefs.

Okay, sometimes I do take center stage.

The problem with liming beliefs is that they are beliefs... that is, you *believe* them. That makes them not only very difficult to challenge and overcome, but even harder to identify. Here are several things you can do to begin identifying your own self-limiting beliefs:

- **Monitor your negative self-talk**
  Keep track of the times you hold yourself back with negative self-talk. Negative self-talk takes the form of phrases such as
  I'm not good at…
  I could never…
  I don't deserve…
  People like me don't…
  These phrases reveal deeply held beliefs about yourself and your situation. For two weeks, keep track of the number of times phrases like these creep into your thoughts. This is not a time to shut down or act against those thoughts; this is a time to monitor and keep track of them. What commonalities arise among them? What do these instances say about what you think about yourself?
- **Think about patterns in your life**
  We humans are really good at making the same mistakes over and over again. We like to think we learn from those mistakes, but sometimes we don't. Chances are, there are some unfounded limiting beliefs underlying these patterns. Look for patterns in your own life, especially patterns that frustrate or confuse you. Write them down and look for the common threads that seem to connect them. Look for

times when you were able to break that pattern, either by your own will or the influence of external forces. What was different about those times?

- **Challenge your assumptions**
  When you find yourself predicting an outcome before a thing takes place—for example, assuming you will or won't get a job you are thinking of applying for, or assuming that your partner will respond a certain way to an idea you have—dig into those assumptions and challenge them. Ask yourself:

    o Is that objectively true and 100% certain?
    o Where and how did I learn that assumption?
    o Who benefits from this assumption, and how?
    o What would someone else say about this assumption?

- **Check your *shoulds* and *musts***
  Any time you hear yourself say, "I should" or "I must," pause a moment and ask yourself, "Why?" *Should* and *must* are masking words because they often hide a false, limiting belief under the mask of unquestionable authority. "I should skip my kid's soccer game for this meeting" and "I should skip this meeting for my kid's soccer game" are both equally valid and equally questionable statements. The same questions you would ask to challenge your assumptions can be applied to the *shoulds* and *musts* in your life. Who

benefits or profits from these unquestionable *musts*? What would happen if I disobeyed the *shoulds*?

- **Seek external evidence and perspectives**
  An external assessment and a professional opinion can go a long way to identifying your self-limiting beliefs. The most difficult thing about a limiting belief is that you believe it. That makes is almost impossible to identify. A fish does not know it's wet. Not only does it have no concept of *dry*, it has no way of imagining *dry*. The fish exists in its environment. And so it is with humans. We exist in our own environment, and we lack the ability to see that environment from an external perspective. Working with a professional or simply checking in with others can give you perspectives you can't give yourself.

It's quite likely that you are the biggest obstacle to having the fulfilling life you want. Your own limiting beliefs about yourself, about other people, or about the situation may be clouding your ability to see possibility and to take actions you need to take.

Section 2

Light the Path

Every minute of every day, you make decisions that create your future. From decisions as large as saying yes or no to a marriage proposal, to decisions as small as choosing the apple or the cookie for your mid-afternoon snack, each choice you make shapes not just how your life will go in the future, but who you are becoming.

In this section, you'll gain new perspective that will help you

- Get more emotionally close to your future self,
- Understand how you may be betraying your future self, and
- Be more intentional about choosing courage in the little moments.

Reflect on the self-awareness you built in the last section. What insights did you find as you went through the exrercises?

What new questions are you asking yourself as you think about going into the next section of this book?

Your Future Self is a Demanding Micromanager

You're reading this book right now because you care about the happiness of your future self, but really? You probably don't have a very good relationship with your future self. That's because your future self is a demanding micromanager.

As a professional coach, I focus a lot on the idea of your future self. Clarifying goals, understanding strengths, focusing on core values, creating plans, moving to action, changing behavior—these are all things we work on to move from where we are today to where we want to be. I help my clients envision, define, and clarify the person they want to be in the future, and make plans on how to get there. These things take time; it's not like flipping a switch and suddenly you have a fulfilling life *right now*. You're creating a fulfilling life for your future self.

But the term *future self* is muddier than it seems on the surface because your future self *is not you*. It turns out that the human brain thinks of the future self as if it's a completely different person from the current self. That is, the parts of your brain that light up when you think about your future self are the same parts that light up when you think about other people. In other words, in your own mind, future-you is not you. Future-you is somebody else.

Depending on how emotionally close you are to your future self (it varies from person to person), you might think of that person like you think of an acquaintance in the workplace, or perhaps like the hotel clerk when you're on vacation. Thus, when making decisions, you consider the effects of your choices on future-you in the same way you consider the effects of your choices on that colleague, or on the hotel desk clerk.

Yet as sure as there is a clerk at the hotel's front desk, there is a future you doing future-you things, struggling with future-you problems, and feeling future-you emotions. Unlike the hotel desk clerk, though, that future-you is profoundly affected by current-you decisions. Because of this, future-you may examine, judge, and criticize every decision current-you makes. Your future-you may be the most demanding, micromanaging boss you've ever encountered. How are you supposed to get emotionally close to that kind of jerk?

Let's step back a minute and make an important distinction. I'm actually talking about two different future selves.

First, there's the *aspirational future self*. This is the person you hope to become and are working on becoming—happy, successful, well-loved, fulfilled, comfortable… whatever words you would use to describe where you want to be. It's good to have aspirations, and it's good to set those aspirations high.

Second, there's the *actual future self*. This is the person you become in the future regardless of your aspirations. This person is the result of all the choices you make and the things that happen to you. This is who you will become regardless of what you aspire to today.

In the first part of this book, you did a lot of work to describe who you are today. The next step, of course, is to describe your *aspirational future self*. Who do you aspire to be? What do you aspire that your life will look like? If you haven't done that yet, you might take some time right now, before moving on to the next paragraph, to at least jot down some notes.

Great! Now that you've described your *aspirational future self*, you can map the steps that will get you there. Take a few minutes to describe the gaps between where you are today and the aspirations you've just articulated. This is basic change management—describe the current state, describe the future state, and create an action plan to bridge the gap between the two. This is how you map your action plan from *current self* to *aspirational future self*.

Done? Fantastic. And, *voila!* Now there's a new person out there who expects you to show up on time, dedicate yourself completely and totally to this new action plan, and successfully accomplish every one of the steps you just laid out. Because this new action plan is not actually *your* plan. It's *aspirational future self's* plan.

And now *aspirational future self* is breathing down your neck like a narcissistic, micromanaging boss.

Aspirational future self expects you to sacrifice everything for the new plan. Talk about judgment—make one mistake, and you get an instant guilt trip. And, if you actually succeed in sticking to the plan, *actual future self* will end up stealing all the credit. Meanwhile, this *aspirational future self* literally never does anything for you.

You wouldn't stay in a job with that kind of boss, would you? I certainly wouldn't.

I'm guessing you also don't want to *be* that kind of boss. Yet here you are, looking back at your *past self* and judging them for all their mistakes, poor choices, and laziness. You could be so much more right now if your *past self* had just been more disciplined! If only you could go back and whip *past self* into shape, you wouldn't even have to be reading this book and doing all this work. You'd already have the fulfilling life you want. You'd already be everything you should be.

Right about now you might be expecting me to say, "Imagine that micromanaging, demanding *future self* coming back to whip you into shape. That'll get you motivated!"

But I won't say that. Because it wouldn't motivate you any more than having your narcissistic, micro-managing boss hovering over your shoulder and whispering criticisms into your ear would motivate you to work harder or be more skilled. That kind of approach might sound insightful and might feel satisfying and powerful to people who feel a strong need for control, and it might even work in short bursts. But that kind of browbeating is rarely sustainable in real life. In fact, just the opposite; it more often creates feelings of resentment, anger, and detachment. The goal here is to get emotionally closer to your *aspirational future self*, not resentful and filled with rage.

Your *aspirational future self* is such a demanding micromanager because their existence literally depends on you following through with the action plan. If you fail to execute to the plan, that version of *aspirational future self* will never exist. A different future self will exist. And that's okay.

Every day, from moment to moment, we make choices. Each of those choices is made by our current self, according to current motivations, current values, current context, and current external pressures. These choices create your actual future self regardless of your aspirations, hopes, desires, or intentions. What happens is that your *actual future self* and your *aspirational future self* either diverge or converge.

It's like walking across a desert with your goal being a mountain peak 10,000 steps away. Your *aspirational future self* lives on that mountaintop. If you take one step every second, you will without doubt be somewhere after 10,000 seconds. But, depending on which direction you take each step, you may or may not end up on top of that particular mountain peak.

The goal should be lofty.

Aspirational future self looks down from that peak in judgment and fear, throwing feelings of shame and inadequacy at you. If you try to look back at the steps you've taken, *aspirational future self* only points out missteps and mistakes, never recognizing how far you've actually come. Make enough steps in the wrong direction—it doesn't have to be very many—and soon that mountain peak where *aspirational future self* sits may seem entirely unreachable. Even if each of those steps resulted in great joy, financial windfall, or wonderful relationships, you might still feel so much guilt from *aspirational future self* that you can't appreciate any of that success. Instead, your current self just judges and shames your past self.

It's a terrible loop. But it's not an inevitability. You can break that loop right now.

This is real life. Things change. On the journey of 10,000 steps, you might find that your goals change, or context changes, or you have new responsibilities or aspirations or hopes or disabilities. Some of these are outside your control, like your employer going out of business or your parent suddenly requiring you to be their caregiver. Some are choices you must wrestle with. Although the *aspirational future self* you envision might represent your authentic hopes right now in this moment, it's okay to rethink things as change happens. And if you find that the *aspirational future self* you're envisioning right now is different from the dream you had in the past, that's okay, too. This is how you break the cycle of self-judgment: start by being kind and forgiving to your past self. Look back at the 10,000 steps you've taken so far, and appreciate how far you've come. Recognize the successes, the growth, the obstacles overcome, and all the other positives from that journey. Specifically, work on these things:

- **Forgive your past self for all their missteps**
  Your past self was doing the best they could, without the benefit of the hindsight you now have. Give them a break. Focusing on choices they made using *current self* context is simply unfair. Don't be that judgmental micromanager to your past self. Be better than that. If you can do that today, then your future self will probably also be less of a judgmental micromanager to your current self.

- **Recognize how far you've come**
  Now that you've stopped focusing on *past self's* mistakes, look at how far *past self* has come. Look at the joy, relationships, and success they built along the way. Even if things have gone horribly wrong and there's very little to celebrate in your past, I guarantee there is something of value to highlight. If there wasn't, it's highly unlikely that you would be this far into this book. Instead of judging each past misstep, praise each positive outcome, even if it wasn't the intended outcome.

- **Be intentional about each new decision**
  Whenever you have a choice to make, be intentional about it. Everything from what you'll have for breakfast, to whether you'll quit your current job. If you can articulate how this decision moves you toward the mountain peak or toward a new destination, you are likely to be more intentional about your choice.

- **Don't give up all your power to the original *aspirational future self***
  Absolutely ask *aspirational future self* what they think of the choice you're about to make and how you're progressing. After all, at one point you decided that *aspirational future self* was who you really wanted to become. But don't give that original aspiration too much power. Don't let it beat you down. Just like you can quit working for a narcissistic micromanager, you can kick that original *aspirational future self* to the curb and re-envision the future.
- **Bring *future self* closer to you**
  People tend to execute on their plans more reliably when they are emotionally close to their future self. This may mean that you need to do some work to make good friends with that person, or it may mean that you need to reduce the scope of your plans—stop aiming for the mountaintop and choose a series of much closer destinations. The smaller the change, the easier it is to achieve.

Personally, I find it liberating to know that I think of my future self as a different person from who I am today. It gives me the room to understand that my past self was also different, and to forgive myself for past mistakes. It also allows me to accept that I will change in the future, and that those around me will also change. This means that my future self is not an immutable ideal, but a real person that will come to be whether I intend it or not. This gives me room to make future mistakes, and that's when creativity and growth can occur.

The future will happen no matter what I choose to do, so I should be intentional about each choice. That's a powerful thought. Being intentional about choices requires a commitment to increasing your self-awareness, and to refreshing your situational awareness constantly.

Life is short. The journey of 10,000 steps is about whatever step your current self takes right now, as informed by the steps before and the intended destination. You don't actually know how many steps you will get to take in the future, so don't you want to be happy with where you are right now, and not just in some imagined future?

In Martinez, California

Finding Contentment

A year ago, the path was clear.
I aimed for There and started Here.
So I went forth without delay
to turn my Here to Far Away.
But as I went, each There became
another Here, each one the same.
At every Here I turned around
to see the last Here that I'd found.
I saw that Now had changed to Then
and wanted to go There again.
But this is Now and Here I'll stay,
for There is just too Far Away.

How You Betray Your Future Self

There are times in my life that I've told myself "no" when I had the opportunity to do something new or interesting. I don't remember those times. What I remember are the things that happened because I said "yes." Like how I went bowling at the White House because I taught myself HTML 20 years earlier.

Well, it might not have been exactly that straight a line. Allow me to explain.

A little over 25 years ago, I indulged a bit of whimsical folly that changed my life in wholly unexpected ways. On December 9th, 1997, I secured the domain name peterdudley.com. In those days, domain names were free, Google hadn't been founded yet, and the <blink> tag was considered fun and innovative. At that time, I was working in tech, and the "world wide web" was a hot, new topic for entrepreneurs. So, it wasn't a huge stretch for me to jump in and learn all I could, in much the same way artificial intelligence is enticing people today.

I didn't have any kind of plan for this new interest, though. I had a vague sense that it might make me more marketable, or that I might be able to start my own dot-com. Or, as Newsweek had declared around that time with a cover article claiming the internet was merely a passing fad, I might simply waste a lot of time on nothing.

Building a website was a major undertaking in 1997. Today you can do it in minutes, and the only knowledge you need is how to use a credit card. But back in 1997, you had to understand not just how to code HTML by hand, but also how to install an Apache web server and MySQL database on your own Linux instance. Since all those products were just a few years old, it was a sort of mystical, dark magic. It could take weeks of work and rework and hair-pulling just to get to "hello world."

At a time when I had a new baby, a new home, and a new job, it seemed insane to also start a new, immersive hobby. And yet, if I hadn't, my life would have gone very differently. Here's how getting my domain name led to going bowling at the White House:

- Getting the domain peterdudley.com started me off on learning how to build web applications.
- Later that year, I got laid off and quickly landed a job as a lead web developer at a different startup, largely due to those new skills.

- When that startup folded, these growing skills got me hired to build a web-based application at Wells Fargo focused on corporate social responsibility.
- Seven years later, I was promoted to lead that group and given the responsibility for running several of the company's global employee engagement programs.
- In that role in 2016, I attended a conference in Washington, DC. I was one of about 25 people invited to attend a VIP reception at the White House's bowling alley.

That history is not at all a straight line from point A to point B, and I wouldn't recommend planning your career based on that kind of path. That said, I'm quite certain I never would have arrived at point B if I hadn't let myself explore point A in the first place.

Seriously, the White House bowling alley.

For busy people with demanding jobs, romantic relationships to nurture, homes to maintain, children to raise, aging parents to care for, and any number of other obligations, it's often far too easy to say "no" to yourself. I'm sure I've said no to my own desires countless times over the years, and I'm sure I had very good reasons each time.

I don't remember those times. What I remember are the times I didn't say no. Here are five of those times:

- **Teaching myself web development**
  It would have been easy to put this off because I had a new home, a new baby, and a full-time job, but this untested hobby grew into a whole new career direction.
- **Founding (and abandoning) a startup**
  A friend and I wrote a business plan, formed a corporation, and pitched venture capital firms. We got some traction, but we ended up abandoning it. I learned a lot about myself, business planning, and the world of tech startups.
- **Writing a novel in a month**
  In my early 30s, I started writing fiction again after a decade away from it. I had started and abandoned several novels. Then I heard of this thing called "national novel writing month," and I committed to writing a full novel in the month of November. I could easily have said no, but I accomplished it. Since then, I've written more than a dozen full-length manuscripts.
- **Going on an epic vacation**
  It was more expensive than we could rationally afford, and I'd traveled all over for work, so it would have been easy to

say "no" to an eight-day family trip to Nepal. It turned out even more breathtaking, amazing, and eye-opening than I'd hoped. I will never regret taking that trip.

- **Self-publishing Semper**
  When I nearly quit writing because the publishing industry seemed to be turning into a toxic wasteland, I decided to give self-publishing a try. There was still a stigma attached to self-publishing, and even good friends advised against it. Today, I have my own publishing imprint and am publishing other people's words and art as well as my own.

Some of those things led to major directional shifts in my life, which are still paying dividends for me today. Some of them are just wonderful memories I'm glad to have.

When you think about yourself in 10, 20, or even 50 years, what do you think you'll most remember? What do you *want* to remember? Will you be happier knowing you tried something new without knowing what might come of it? Or would you be happier knowing you dutifully fulfilled all the obligations you had, to the sacrifice of what you wanted at the time? I'm not saying one is better than the other. In fact, I'm against leaning too far either way—there are times for both.

It can be hard to say "yes" to yourself when external pressure or internal self-sabotage is listing out all the reasons to say "no." Here are six reasons I've heard people give for saying "no" to themselves, and how you can overcome them:

1. **You have work to do!**

   Your boss hints that you might get promoted if you work more hours. Your partner wants you to clean up the overgrown yard. Your kids need you to help with homework. Your mom needs you to take her to an appointment. When other people demand your time, there's only one person who will look out for your boundaries: you. Everyone else will take as much as you're willing to give… not because they're mean or selfish, but simply because you're willing to give it. It's up to you to decide how much you're willing to give to other people's agendas. And it's up to you to understand what you need to get in return, if anything.

2. **I have work to do!**

   You're needed at work, and you could get promoted if you work more. The yard really needs to be cleaned up. You should be helping with your kids' homework. You should be a better child to your aging parents. When you define your own value by how much you're needed by others, choosing to say "yes" to your own desires can feel self-indulgent and even self-destructive. Feeling needed boosts the ego so much that often we convince ourselves that others need us more than they actually do. Listen for the language of self-judgment and self-denial in your thoughts. Any time you say "should" to yourself, consider where that thought originates and who really benefits.

3. **That's childish and embarrassing.**

   Whether you love to write poetry, dance in online videos, collect Star Wars figurines, play in a weekend band, or play Dungeons & Dragons, someone somewhere will tell you it's a silly and childish thing. Maybe there's no individual telling you it's silly; maybe it's society making jokes about the trend of pandemic sourdough or the explosion of terrible podcasts. Whatever it is, trying something new just because you're interested in it can bring up feelings of vulnerability and embarrassment. If you've ever stopped yourself because "people will think it's silly," you know what I mean. Find other people who share this interest and start participating in groups where you will find kindred spirits. While you will still have to work on your own self-judgment, being connected with others who share that interest will help.

4. **You can't afford that.**

   When other people tell you how you should and shouldn't spend your money, it means one of two things: Either their personal values are not the same as your personal values, or they're jealous of you for being in control of your own actions. My trip to Nepal was expensive at a time when we should have been saving more for college and paying down our mortgage. People with different priorities might have judged me for spending so much on a trip at that time. Life is a constant series of tradeoff decisions, and how you decide them is up to you.

5. **What a waste of time.**
   That thing you're interested in? It doesn't do anyone any good. You should be doing something valuable and meaningful instead! Volunteer to help homeless people. Go help at a nursing home. Work more hours at your job. Learn a skill someone will pay you for. Stop wasting your time. When people tell you how you should spend your time, they're imposing their own values on you. Achievement culture focuses on return on investment, and there's little or no value placed on fulfillment as a valid return. We oversimplify the idea of value—if we can't immediately see and measure it, then we don't believe it. Yet history is filled with stories of discovery, invention, and enlightenment that started with an idea that had no immediately predictable return. Let your actions and decisions be guided by a combination of your heart, your values, your discernment, and your desire for return. Reframe things to articulate other value you could reap. For example, I never expected to get rich by self-publishing Semper, but I did expect to learn several new skills.

6. **Is this one going to stick?**
   First you bought a guitar. Then you bought a bunch of paints. Then you took up golfing. Then you tried baking. Can't you just settle on something, or are you going to abandon this new thing, too? We have this weird sense that children should try a lot of different things but

grownups should know exactly what we love and pursue it to the exclusion of all else, until the end of time. Some people do, and good for them. Other people never find a single passion. Others learn that their passion is to learn new things. I've felt the embarrassment of abandoning something I told people I was really into. It makes me not want to tell people when I start something new, for fear that I might not stick with it. Then I'd have to explain what a flake I am. If you feel enthusiastic about something, don't betray yourself by abandoning it before you even try it. (Of course, if you live a constant pattern of manic enthusiasm followed by rapid abandonment, you might want to explore that.)

I never thought I'd end up bowling at the White House when I wrote my first HTML code. Maybe I'd have ended up there anyway, but I doubt it. Not even the very wise can see all ends.

I'm glad I had the courage to say "yes" to myself all those times, even amid a loud chorus of "no." Some of the naysaying was external, and some came from within myself. And of course there were other times I did say no to myself. Those times aren't coming to mind at the moment, which is perhaps the biggest lesson from this chapter.

Self-Love

I'm like a dry-erase board
you told me on our first date
nothing's permanent
you can write what you want
insults in violent red
platitudes in blue like the summer sky
green condescensions
*sorrows **black** as grief*

tomorrow I'll wipe it all away
and soak in the freedom
of my own unblemished blankness
free from the sticky residues
of other people

what about love? I remember asking
in what color is love written?

love? you replied
as if startled by the word

why, love is no color at all
love is the eraser
and it took me all my life
to learn how to use it on my own

Be Loyal to Yourself

Telling someone, "Be loyal to yourself" may sound wise and powerful, and that phrase looks great in a meme or on a tee shirt, but what does it even mean, really? It's the kind of vapid verbal scaffolding a self-help guru would give you, then leave the details up to you to figure out. So let's get a little more specific about what it means and why doing it is so hard.

What is loyalty? While a person may be a loyal person—that is, they may value loyalty highly and feel commitment deeply—loyalty is exhibited through behavior and is shown through decision-making. In every moment, for every decision, you are including loyalty among the many personal values factoring into that decision. Absolute loyalty is displayed when someone's core value of *loyalty* wins out over all other values in every decision, regardless of context, situation, and circumstance. Most of us, however, do not live a life of absolute loyalty to anyone or anything, even to ourselves. We live in a world of context, situation, and circumstance; loyalty is simply one of the many factors in play.

Being loyal to yourself does not mean being a narcissistic jerk. That's not loyalty to yourself; it's just selfishness. Being loyal to yourself is very similar to being *authentically you*—honoring the unique person you are, and being committed to that unique person even when doing so is uncomfortable. Sometimes this means choosing yourself over others; sometimes it means sacrificing for a bigger purpose.

Now let's talk about which self you're supposed to be loyal to. Your past self? Your future self? Or some made-up version of yourself that doesn't really exist?

Allow me to illustrate with an example from a writers conference I was working a few years ago. Rachel, one of the conference attendees and an experienced writer of young adult fantasy novels, asked me for advice. She had an exciting idea for a new novel, but it wasn't in her usual genre of young adult fantasy. She asked me if she should write this new book, or if she should forget it and stick with what she'd established her name on.

When she posed this question, she probably expected me to ask what genre this new story was so I could start judging its marketability, the effect it might have on her personal brand, and the complexities of genre-hopping. Instead, I asked her, "Do you feel more loyal to your past self or to your future self?"

She thought a few seconds, then replied, "I feel most loyal to my readers."

"So," I concluded, "your greatest loyalty is to somebody else's made-up version of you."

Rachel's dilemma is not unlike someone thinking of making a career change, or going back to school, or moving across the country, or breaking up with a long-time partner. They're all some version of changing an important and public-facing piece of your personal identity. They all involve some aspect of letting go of the past in order to create a new future.

One of my favorite metaphors for this kind of dilemma is this: *You can't cross the ocean without having the courage to lose sight of the shore.*

Quotes like that can inspire and motivate, especially when turned into memes or put on tee shirts or hung on the wall in your dentist's office. But quotes like that can also trick people into making the wrong decisions for the wrong reasons.

Let's take that quote about the ocean and the shore, for example. It defines courage in a very limited way. Sure, sometimes the most courageous thing to do is to ditch your past and charge into the unknown. But sometimes it takes more courage to return to shore and stay in the life you have now. And sometimes courage isn't the thing that's needed to make the best decisions; sometimes discretion is the better part of valor.

Now let's get back to Rachel. She told me that she felt her greatest loyalty was to her readers. That sounds good, noble, and brand-aware, doesn't it? Perhaps it is. But maybe it's just Rachel capitulating to the overwhelming gravity created by other people's expectation that she is, and always will be, an author of young-adult fantasy novels.

Every day we choose how we show up in the world, and each of those choices, whether we intend it or not, teaches everyone around us who we are. Rachel wrote young-adult fiction. The people who read those books now think of her as a young-adult author. When they see she has a new book out, they'll expect it to be similar to what she's written before.

Some of those people will be selfishly disappointed if it's different from what they expect. They will be angry and will take it personally: *How dare she change my experience?*

Others will simply be skeptical: *She wrote some good young-adult novels, but adult literary fiction is so different. She should stick to what she knows.*

The irony of success is that the more successful you get at something, the harder it can be to change… specifically because of the overwhelming grip that history has on your identity. It becomes harder to lose sight of the shore when everyone else keeps dragging you back to land. Meanwhile, as the skeptics keep pulling you back to shore, your champions will push you relentlessly to make it across that ocean. Skeptics won't think you can succeed. Selfish people will expect you to always stay exactly as they want you to be. Your champions and cheerleaders will pressure you to move forward, even if moving forward turns out to be wrong for you.

Rachel's idea that she is most loyal to her readers is a bit like that quote about losing sight of the shore. *Loyalty to her readers* defines *readers* in narrow terms—the people who have already discovered her and read her existing novels. These are the people pulling her back to shore. But would it be more courageous to try the new book and find new readers, or to ditch the thing she's so excited about in service to those who know her?

When you're most loyal to someone else's version of you, you may end up betraying yourself. You may be pulled back to shore when you really want to cross the ocean, or you may be pushed out to sea when you really want to return to shore.

Contemplating any kind of major change brings to the surface any conflicts you may be feeling between your intrinsic values (who you want to become) and external pressures (who others tell you to be). These conflicts can manifest in many ways, and getting past them to the right decision can be difficult, confusing, and painful. There's often quite a lot of ambivalence to navigate, and even when you reach a decision you may find the second-guessing to be just as difficult, confusing, and painful.

When you're in this kind of ambivalence spin, asking this simple question might help clarify some of the ambiguity or shake loose some of those stubborn and pesky limiting beliefs: Are you most loyal to your past self, to your future self, or to some fictitious self that's been created by others?

None of those is always the correct answer. None of those is always the wrong answer. The right answer depends on all the same factors that go into the decision of whether to change or not. Sometimes a simple reframing of the question in this way will make the answer unavoidably obvious. Not always, but it happens more than you might think.

When you're in touch with your core values and understand the external pressures influencing you, you can thoughtfully weigh each of these with intentionality and clarity. And that leads to the best decision-making.

What is one way you may be holding yourself back by being loyal to a previous version (or the current version) of you?

What is one way you can be more loyal to your aspirational future self?

Avoid Identity Creep

As I've pointed out throughout this book, you make small decisions all day long, every day. Each of those decisions plays some role in who you are becoming and how you're shaping your future. Over time, all these small decisions add up.

In your journey of 10,000 steps, each step moves you in some direction. If you're not intentional about deciding which direction to take each step—or even if you are intentional but you compromise on your values—you may look up one day and wonder, *How the hell did I get here? Who is this person I see in the mirror?* You may feel so far off course that you can't even remember what the original course was. That's identity creep: the slow erosion of who you are through lots of little compromises and decisions that nudge you in the wrong direction.

Anything we fear (losing a job, losing a contract, losing a marriage), anything we desire (prestige, fame, money, influence), or anything we need (food, shelter) can present dilemmas that force us to choose between competing values, fears, needs, and desires. If we're not checking in with ourselves, or we stop looking for our north star, or we don't have someone else to check ourselves against, we may fall into the trap of "I'll just compromise on my values this time" or "I'll just cut this corner this time." I've seen this in people (including myself), and I've seen this in the startups, nonprofits, and Fortune 100 companies I've worked for. All you have to do is look at the news to see it.

How you make each choice reveals who you are. But each choice you make also influences who you become. This is why something like a pandemic or turning 50 or losing a sibling or being abandoned by your peers can knock you sideways. Events like these often make people see themselves in a different light, and they don't always like who they've become.

When people aren't in touch with who they are at their core, they put themselves at risk of identity creep: They slowly become a manifestation of the accumulation of other people's opinions, fears, and desires instead of who they really are inside.

I'm a realist. There are big gray areas where courage and foolhardiness overlap, where fear and discretion overlap, where paranoia and concern overlap. Identity creep happens in those gray areas. External pressures can be overwhelming. It can feel impossible to break away and do something different from what everyone else expects and demands of you. Sometimes it's just not safe or realistic to do what your heart tells you. Some decisions have no good options. Some situations have no good outcomes. And frequently, even when we're in touch with our core values, we face complex decisions where multiple values we hold dear are in conflict.

So, I'm not trying to say that if you just stick tightly to your values, everything will always work out okay. What I am saying is that every time you make a decision that goes against who you are at your core, you nudge yourself farther away from happiness. You nudge yourself toward a situation where you feel perpetually out of place, never truly fitting the life you're living.

So how can you avoid identity creep, or correct it when you recognize you've let it happen to you? Here are four deceptively simple tips. They sound easy on the surface, but they can take a lot of work and constant diligence to incorporate into your lifestyle.

1. **Surround yourself with the right people**

    Some people with their own agendas will try to manipulate you into decisions that go against who you are. They want to change you into their vision of you rather than accept you for who you are. Surround yourself with people who see and support you, and avoid entangling with people who treat you as a secondary character in their own adventure. Also, don't be one of those people to someone else.

2. **Filter out the "helpful" noise**

    Not everyone who gives you advice is trying to manipulate or change you. Well-meaning, supportive people who have your best interests at heart will tell you what they think is best. You need to become profoundly self-aware and in tune with your own value system in order to know what of that is useful and what is just noise you should ignore. Also, when you give someone you care for advice, allow them the room to reject it.

3. **Engage in creative and critical thinking**

   When it seems there aren't any options, force yourself to be creative. Don't fall into the trap of single-issue decision making, which can have you chasing a red herring. When you can step back from the situation, name your fears and desires, separate facts from opinions, and expand your imagination, you may find that the best option is one you hadn't yet thought of.

4. **Choose courage in the little moments**

   Identity creep happens in the gray areas and the little conflicts, and it reveals itself in the big conflicts. Every decision, no matter how large or how small, defines who you're becoming. In those little conflicts, the moments when it seems a lot easier just to give in rather than do what you know is right, choose courage instead of least resistance. If you can muster the fortitude to choose courage in those moments that seem inconsequential, you'll find it a lot easier to stand confident in your opinions and decisions during in the big conflicts.

Define Your Fulfilling Life

Everyone wants a fulfilling life. They may say it in different ways, but the word *fulfilling* always applies. What five words describe a *fulfilling life* to you? As I write this chapter right now, I would use these five words:

- creative
- peaceful
- connected
- humorous
- balanced

Ask me in a week, and I might change one or two of those words. Directionally speaking, however, these are pretty much how it's going to be for this season of my life. When I was in my teens and learning about life, I would have come up with a different set of words. So, too, in my 20s when I was newly married and beginning my career. Then in my 30s as I became a parent. And again in my 40s, when I was writing novels, making my mark professionally, and parenting a teen with suicidal depression. Now, in my mid 50s with so many things changing, I'm looking at a very different definition of a "fulfilling life."

I feel keenly in touch with what is meaningful to me. I understand my own purpose, my own definitions of success, and how coaching and writing and publishing fulfill me every day. I feel very fortunate to feel this way; it seems there's a growing epidemic of people feeling lost, stuck, or untethered—all words new clients have used when they first tell me they need a life change of some kind but don't know what.

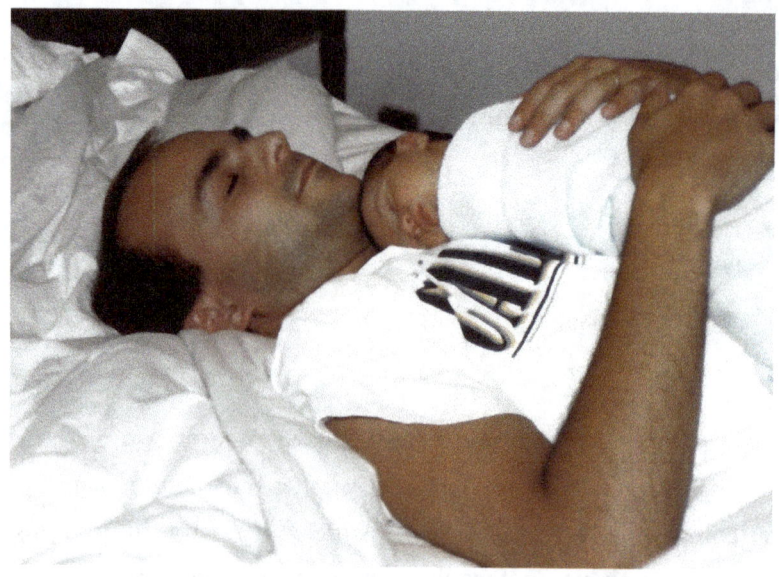

Fulfillment at age 30. But if I'm honest? Not so much at age 57.

Define Your Fulfilling Life | 75

When you're trying to describe your fulfilling life, you need to get very clear on what you really want. To do that, you must do three things:

1. Ignore what others think you should want

If you're stuck in someone else's definition of fulfillment, you may feel like a failure or always end up disappointed. You feel like you're on the wrong track, even though all the *shoulds* tell you you're doing life right. For example, when I ask my older clients about the life they look forward to in retirement, nearly everyone includes "travel" among their desires. For most, that's a default answer. After all, doesn't everyone want to travel in retirement? But few can readily explain what it is about "travel" they find fulfilling. Adventure? Personal growth? Inspiration? A glamorous lifestyle? Escape?

Are those the same words they would use to describe the fulfillment they imagine for the coming season of their life? How about when no one else is listening? That is, when they separate their own intrinsic desires from what they think their peers, their family members, their coworkers, and their community expect them to want. Most of us spend so much of our lives negotiating externally imposed value systems that by the time we get to a certain age, we've forgotten how to listen just to ourselves. Some of us have even forgotten how to want something for ourselves, having allowed our identity to creep so much that we now only see ourselves as a secondary character in other people's lives.

In my case, writing, editing, and publishing are all important parts of my fulfilling life. In particular, creating the book RELIT hit most of my five fulfillment words. While I would love to sell ten million copies and be interviewed on NPR and Colbert, those things are not necessary for my life to feel fulfilling and complete.

2. *Rethink what you used to want*

Periods of transition are hard. As you move from one season of life to another, you need to look forward to what will be fulfilling in your new season and let go of what you used to find fulfilling. When I blew out my knee (the second time), I had to come to peace with the idea that my amateur soccer career was over. It had been an integral part of my joy, my health routine, and my community. Without soccer available to me, I had to embrace new ways of being joyful, keeping healthy, and finding community.

Recently, I spoke with a client who is in that slow transition from "parent of children" to "parent of adults." It's a transition many parents aren't trained for, so as their children eagerly try to break free and become independent, the parents feel pulled apart. They cling to past ideas of what being a parent meant (intentionally or unintentionally) instead of embracing their new situation. They slip into frustration and resentment, and their children pull away even more aggressively.

If these parents think deeply and honestly about what a *future* fulfilling life would comprise, they will be much more likely to find their clear north star and be more able to envision a positive future. They will look ahead to their parental role as peer-adult and find it easier to let go of their parental role of overseer-guardian. If, however, they get stuck tethered to what made the last season of their lives fulfilling instead of refiguring what a fulfilling life looks like in the future, they're about to face a long period of difficulty, conflict, and resentment.

3. *Think critically about what you admire in others*

One of my coaching go-tos when people are trying to move forward in their careers is to ask them about the people they admire. This can be a tar pit question, though. You can get stuck in a dangerous spot with this one. Why? Because often, the people we admire are the people who have strengths that are different from our own. We admire those people because they seem so effortless with things that we find difficult.

For example, I admire people who exude self-confidence and who can sell with determined tenacity, like one of my old bosses who relished doing battle in the sales arena. He was good at it. He loved it. If I spent my energy trying to emulate him, I would feel like the proverbial fish out of water approximately one hundred percent of the time. I would be in constant discomfort. Success would be elusive. I would not feel I was living a fulfilling life. In fact, just the opposite.

It's good to admire people. But it's important to think critically about what it is you admire about them, and whether that maps to who you are or not. Don't spend your life chasing after the wrong ideals or ignoring your own talents trying to be someone else.

Now, write down your five words

A decade ago, my sister wanted to talk with me about planning out the second half of her life. We never got to have that conversation. I'm now three years older than she ever got to be, and although the realities of existing in a capitalist society impose themselves on me daily (like everyone, I have to earn a living), I am dedicated to living what I consider is a fulfilling life. I don't want to get to my final day, whenever that may be, wishing I could start over or do it all differently.

Don't wait for some time in the future to start living your own fulfilling life. You may miss your one opportunity. Get started right now by writing down the five words that define the fulfilling life you want. Keep this list in a place where you will stumble upon it frequently. When you do, pause a moment and contemplate how you are aligning with that list in the present moment.

1. _____

2. _____

3. _____

4. _____

5. _____

Find Your Own Solutions

Do you want to know how to make someone feel really bad about not being able to get their shit together? Tell them exactly how to get their shit together.

You saw a YouTube video. You read a book. You did a LinkedIn learning. You took a class. Or maybe you came up with it yourself. "I know exactly what you should do," you should say with confidence. Then tell them the thing that worked for you, smirk with smugness at your own brilliance and magnanimity, and watch them try to thank you as they slowly realize the horror that you just unleashed on them.

Most of us have a strong desire to help other people solve problems we've already conquered. After all, if we've found *the solution*, why would we withhold it? Even if we haven't found *the solution*, many people—especially those with long careers in management, teaching, or leadership—feel a pull to jump straight into solutions. We all do it to some extent, mostly when talking with friends, coworkers, or our own children, especially when they've got a problem that we think we know something about.

"I have trouble with time management," someone might say. Most people jump straight to what has worked for them. Their favorite calendar app. Their own personal methodology on managing their to-do list. Their deep and profound commitment to decluttering. Their undeniable faith in having a focus on exercise, mindfulness, or self-empowerment. But there's a fundamental problem in offering people solutions to problems you've already solved. They're *your* solutions, not *their* solutions. Not everyone sees the world as you do. Not everyone experiences the world as you do. One size does not fit all.

Even factors that seem completely unrelated might make your solution ineffective for someone else. Remember the great internet dress controversy of 2015, the one where a photo of a dress looked either blue and black, or white and gold? Different people saw the dress differently, and unlike most optical illusions, this was not a situation where you could trick your brain into seeing the dress the other colors than you saw it at first. I personally see the dress as yellow and white, even though I have read that it is, in fact, blue and black. Why is this relevant?

Some research published in an article in Slate in 2017 suggested a correlation between how you see the dress and what time you go to bed each day. People with late bedtimes saw the dress one way, and people with early bedtimes saw it the other. The author's research (not peer-reviewed science, to my knowledge) showed that people

Find Your Own Solutions | 81

who go to bed late tend to experience more incandescent lighting, and people who go to bed early tend to experience greater natural lighting. Because the brain must fill in a lot of missing context in such a small photo with little additional information, it makes some pretty big assumptions based on what it's already experienced.

When you were arguing with your colleagues about the colors of this dress, did they ask you what time you normally went to bed? Of course not. Besides the threat of potentially getting referred to HR, they didn't know that bedtime might be a key factor in your experience of this photograph. And that's really the point of this chapter: Everyone has their own unique blend of factors that affect how they experience life and the world around them. When someone has found "the solution" to your problem, they're either unaware of or ignoring a whole host of other things that might make their solution a complete flop for you. (Either that, or they're trying to sell you something.)

I talk with clients all the time who have aimlessly and unsuccessfully tried to pick from a litany of "solutions" that friends, family, or self-declared experts have told them to try. They can't settle on any one of those solutions, even though all those people seem so authoritative and successful and confident. Since it worked for those people, it should work for everyone. Right?

As you collect solutions from the people who care about you, it's important to see all those solutions as simply well-intended suggestions. They were valid paths to success for someone, but that doesn't mean they're right for everyone. That's because we all come from different backgrounds. We don't all take in information the same way. We don't process information the same way. We don't all arrange the results the same way. Our brains use complicated, subtle calculations based on our unique experiences and biases to color the world around us.

Gold and white? Or blue and black?

The most insidious thing about experts solutioning for others is that if their solution doesn't work for you, it can actually make you feel worse. It worked for the expert, so if it doesn't work for you then you must be the problem. When you're already swimming in a puddle of self-doubt because of the problem itself, continuously trying and failing at other people's sure-fire solutions just brings on more self-doubt and shame.

That said, if you take in enough suggestions, it's often likely that one of them will turn out to be the actual solution you need. But how do you know which is the best one? Quite simply, the best approach is the one you actually use. Not much else truly matters.

You can pay top price for the most highly rated home gym recommended by all the fitness experts, but if you only use it to hang laundry on, it's not a solution for you. If you actually use the cheap stretch cords every day, then that's the best solution for you. You can buy the most feature-rich calendar app with artificial intelligence and color coding, but if what you actually use is a dry-erase wall calendar while the app never gets opened, which is the better solution?

The best is the one you actually use.

Section 3

Make It So

You've gotten this far, so you're probably eager to start making some changes. Let's get to work. In this section, you'll get inspiration to get started, and you'll learn:

- Techniques to help you keep moving forward,
- How to survive the J Curve, and
- How to live with intention.

Check in with yourself. Review the goals you wrote down on page 2, and adjust them (if necessary) based on the exploration you've done in the intervening 82 pages. What have you learned? What new questions are you asking yourself?

Life's Not a Sprint.
Neither is it a Marathon.

You're eager to get off and running, sure.

I love beginnings. The beginning of a new adventure is aglow with positivity, sparkly with glitter, alive with cheering and back-slapping, and steeped in the heady ozone and sulfur of just-exploded fireworks. I always start out strong, with big goals. I can see the mountaintop from the starting line. I'm like Caractacus Potts envisioning the gleaming, magical Chitty Chitty Bang Bang in the dirty old junker. I get seduced by possibility, like so many of us do when starting a new project.

Getting to the finish line is another thing, though

I came across a photograph when I was downsizing my life a few years ago. The picture was taken in 1986. In it, I am crossing the finish line of the Bay to Breakers, an iconic 12K race through the streets of San Francisco which starts along the edge of the Bay and finishes beside the Pacific Ocean. I look exhausted in this photo.

I am a freshman in college. I am wearing my jersey from my high school track team, which I still have but cannot fit into.

Here's what I remember about that race: I start out strong. I'm cruising, keeping pace with far more experienced runners. I'm young and fit. This is great. I'm keeping up with them for four or five miles before I start to get tired. And then, when I think we're five miles into the 7 1/2 mile run, I see the first signpost.

One mile.

That's not one mile left to go. That's one mile *done*. Shit.

Talk about feeling dejected. My earnest naïveté got me so excited that when I got to that first mile marker I felt almost like a failure, even though I'd barely begun. Could I even finish the other 6 1/2 miles? Well, not only did I finish the run, I made the top 5,000 (barely) and got my name in the paper. Still, I felt like a fool. I had let my excitement run ahead of my reason. No doubt that fast start helped me finish as high in the rankings as I did, but if I had to do it over again, I would have been much more evenly paced and enjoyed the experience a lot more.

I've noticed this pattern in myself through other projects and life phases. I get excited about an idea, do the bare minimum of planning, and jump into making it real right away. After a short time, though, I begin to doubt myself. Success seems farther away than it felt at first. The work seems more of a grind when I'm in the middle of it. I get discouraged. I want to always see the sparklers, hear the cheering, smell the fireworks. Don't we all?

People love to share the meme that says, "Life is a marathon, not a sprint." But rarely is it truly one or the other. Of the five novels I've published, exactly one of them was a sprint, written in a single month. The others took more than a year each. None was a marathon, either. Each was more like a series of sprints and jogs and rests, with plenty of wrong turns and backtracking along the way.

I'd like to say that no one ever told me it would be so difficult to find my own process through these big projects. That I may have to start, change tactics, start again, persevere, and on and on. But I'm sure I'd been told. Probably hundreds of times, in myriad ways.

People love to say "No one ever told me…" when they learn from experience how hard something is. No one ever told me parenting would be so hard! No one ever told me I'd feel like a failure halfway through writing my novel! No one ever told me writing a blog post every week would be a challenge!

The truth is, everyone who's ever done those things has told us. Over and over and over. It's just that we have to experience it for ourselves, sometimes, to actually understand it. And that's what I'm telling you now. You must find your own process that works for you in this new phase of your life. There is no single solution that will work equally well for everyone who picks up this book.

So, get ready to figure it out. It's not a sprint. It's not a marathon. It's your own journey, at your own pace.

88 | Take Your Time | Dudley

"Someday" is not in this calendar.

Someday is Not a Date on the Calendar

The speaker at the 2024 writers conference looked out over the hundreds of attendees and told us, "Someday is not a date on the calendar." It hit home for me, and for most of the people in the audience. I'd heard that bit of fridge magnet wisdom before, of course. But it's good to be reminded from time to time, especially in those moments when you've got a chance to take action.

Everyone has a someday thing. Some of us have several. Someday I'm going to write a book. Someday I'm going to get a master's degree. Someday I'm going to ask for a raise. Someday I'm going to try to reconcile with my father. Someday I'm going to start my own business.

But someday is always in the future. It's never today. It's also not tomorrow. Nor next Tuesday. It's not June 5th, or the winter solstice, or your 58th birthday. There is no date labeled "someday" on your calendar. Go ahead and check.

What is your someday thing? I think everyone should have at least one. You know it in your heart, but maybe you've been keeping it secret because telling other people will make it real. Or maybe you've been telling everyone for decades, and no one believes you anymore. Including you.

I used to think of myself as a dreamer, not a doer. But when I look back over my life, the evidence shows that I've done a pretty good job of pursuing my somedays. Better than average, perhaps. One of my someday dreams growing up was "Someday I will be a published author." Today I have my name on more than 10 books, six of which I'm the sole author. I've won awards. I've published other people's words. I've helped people earn the coveted "best seller" merit badge.

Not everyone is so good at pursuing their someday things, though. Over the years, I've noticed patterns in clients, friends, and colleagues that keep them from making their someday things real. If your someday thing is perpetually in the future, you may be falling into one of these three common traps:

1. *You're looking too far ahead*

If you only place value on the end result and not on the steps it takes to get there, then you may never take even that first step. It will always feel like the commitment to start is too daunting. The solution: find value in each of the steps along the way. I'm not just talking about breaking down the big task into approachable milestones. That's basic project management. Breaking down the huge task into segments is only half the solution. You still need to find your motivation for each of those segments. That means finding joy or a sense of accomplishment in the milestones, or joy in the process itself, or someone who will ruthlessly push you along.

The people at the writers conference all found joy in the act of writing. They wrote chapter after chapter, networked, and signed up for classes. But for every person who attended the conference, there are thousands who had the same dream but never even wrote one chapter because they did not find the writing of a single chapter a worthwhile task in itself. They look at writing that chapter as a chore, not as a valuable or enjoyable way to spend their time.

For each of the tasks that go into accomplishing your someday thing, answer these questions:

- What will I learn from this task?
- What will I have accomplished by doing this task?
- How will I feel about myself after finishing this task?

If you can't find the inherent motivation to complete the next milestone, do you care enough about getting to the finish line to struggle through this step? This is as true for starting your own business as it is for learning to dance as it is for writing a book.

2. Something else keeps taking your time

"I just need to prioritize it." How often have you heard yourself say this about a big dream you have but just never seem to get around to? I believe there's truth in the idea that we make time for the things that are truly important to us. If you're never actually doing the thing, then how important can it really be to you?

I like to ask my clients some version of "Imagine you've achieved your someday thing. You did it! Hooray! Now, what role do you see it playing in your life? How is it part of your identity?"

If your someday thing is not truly part of your personal identity, then perhaps it's just fantasy cosplay. What you're drawn to is the trappings of the thing, not the thing itself. It's fun to think about accepting a Grammy, but who wants to do all that rehearsing and performing? It's fun to think about being a published author, but who wants to do all that writing and editing?

If your someday thing is truly a part of who you are in your very soul, then you should be able to find time for it, at least in small bits and pieces. I wrote an entire trilogy while working a full-time job, volunteering as both a scout leader and soccer coach, raising two kids, and fixing up a home... among other things. I was able to do all that not because I'm better than everyone else but because writing is part of who I am at my core. It was profoundly meaningful to me to finish those books. I found the time, even among all my other important priorities.

3. *You're working on it but never getting anywhere*

I love the term "productive procrastination," and I hate when I realize I've been doing it. Productive procrastination is when you are choosing tasks that feel productive but which are far less important than what you really should be doing. For example, reading blog posts about starting your dream business feels like you're investing time and energy toward your goal, but it's not actually creating your business. You will never have a business if you don't actually start your business. You can't finish your someday thing if you don't do the work required to finish the someday thing. When people ask how it's going and you have little progress to show for all the work you've put in, you may be letting yourself fall into a trap of productive procrastination.

Reject the idea that it's about fear

When I talk to new clients who can't seem to make progress on their goals, they frequently jump to "fear of failure" as the reason. I think that's a cop-out. It's an easy answer to a very complex question: Who are you, really?

A lot of people carry around their someday thing like a favorite teddy bear. By saying they will someday be X, that allows them to identify as X without actually having to achieve X. And yet, when they deeply and honestly examine their identity, they may find they don't truly want that someday thing after all. Or, they are unable to achieve it due to things outside their control. Or worse, the reality of it doesn't match their fantasy, and they'd rather give up the dream.

No one wants to lose their favorite teddy bear. So it becomes easier to keep saying "someday" than to give yourself a hard, long look and decide whether "someday" should become either a firm date on the calendar, or "never."

If you're ready to move forward and finally create your fulfilling life, today is the day to make that commitment.

Write that commitment to yourself on the back of this page.

SMART goals (Specific, Measurable, Achievable, Relevant, and Time-Bound) are great for action planning. What time-bound commitment are you making to yourself right now? Make it specific, measurable, achievable, and relevant. And put a date on it.

You're Most Likely to Fail, So What's Stopping You?

Pay attention to the inspirational memes and posts that come through your social media this month. The stories that get told and retold are the ones about success. Often, unusual successes. Stories like these: Julia Child didn't start her culinary career until she was in her 50s. Alan Rickman didn't have his first major film success until 41.

But those are the notable exceptions. A lot of people start cooking later in life and don't end up with their own TV shows. A lot of people pursue acting later in life but don't end up in two of the most popular Christmas movies ever. And a lot of people who want to cook, act, paint, write, sing, or even just change careers later in life never actually do it. Many of them blame "fear of failure," but I think most people don't really understand what they mean by that.

Since the only benchmarks for success we celebrate are stories like Julia Child's and Alan Rickman's, people don't adequately think through what success and failure would look like for their own dreams. What rarely gets talked about is how much of success comes from luck, timing, and connections. Skill and tenacity are necessary ingredients for success, but they're not sufficient. Not even true genius is sufficient. You also need to be lucky.

All you people who are about to shout, "I make my own luck," simmer down. You don't. The very definition of luck is that it's not something you control. If you're successful, you had a lot of help along the way, whether by birth, by timing, by privilege of your demographics, or by luck. There are plenty of geniuses just as skilled and tenacious as you but simply less lucky. The only thing that is truly in your control is your own effort.

When you create a thing, the only outcome that's guaranteed is that you have created the thing. You can't guarantee your novel will get published, or that you'll land an acting role, or that your consultancy will get any clients, or that your cupcakes will be loved far and wide, or that your social media posts will go viral. You can take steps to improve the chance of those outcomes, but there is no way to guarantee any of them. In fact, the odds are stacked against you. You already know this. But you can't win if you don't play. You already know that, too.

So why do you spend your creative energy promising you'll do the thing and then beating yourself up for never actually doing it? Why don't you spend that creative energy doing the thing instead? I have some hypotheses based on personal experience combined with observations of clients, friends, and acquaintances over the last 30 years.

You're Most Likely to Fail | 97

Award winning and best-selling.

1. **You haven't defined what success means for you**
   We all dream of hitting it big, but most of us, in our hearts, don't actually need to hit the best-seller list or win an Emmy or have a million followers to feel happy and fulfilled. It's crucial to figure out what your own definition of success is. Otherwise, you'll be trapped in overwhelm at how impossible it is to "succeed" according to society's measure.

2. **Vulnerability and fear of being judged**
   Few things strike a person's deep vulnerabilities like artistic expression. When you create something new from your own imagination—a poem, a painting, a song, a business—you feel intimately exposed. The judgments that follow can feel intensely personal. It's important to recognize this and be intentional about either accepting the vulnerability and going for it, or deciding it's more than you're willing to risk.

3. **Paralyzed by fear of wasting time/money/effort**

   The types of pursuits I'm talking about require a significant investment in time, money, or effort. But we live in a society obsessed with return on investment, so if you can't articulate the ROI of your thing, then other responsibilities always seem more important. This overdeveloped need for productivity may keep pushing your dream—which we know is doomed to fail by ROI standards—to the bottom of the list. If you are ever going to start, you have to get okay with investing in yourself, with the only certain return being your happiness.

4. **Staying in "creator mode"**

   A friend recently complained that they have started 16 novels but never finished even one. They felt like a failure. But I think they just really like being in creator mode. Why should finishing be the measure of success? If you love tinkering, then tinker. If you want to finish, then finish. Either way is fine; there is no need to be so judgy of yourself.

5. **Staying in "dreamer" mode**

   While it's true that you can't win if you don't play, it's also true that you can't lose if you don't play. Having a dream is a lovely state to be in, but the dream dies the day you begin to pursue it. It moves out of the realm of fantasy and into reality. Some people just want to stay in the fantasy. And that's okay.

6. **It may not actually be your dream**

   I am fond of saying that we make time for what is important. By that I mean that how you spend your time reveals what you believe to be important. If you say you want to do something but never seem to find the time for it, you may need to reexamine how much it truly means to you… as opposed to how much you like to think it means to you. It may be that you're caught up in the perceived identity—there is a writing group I participate in that promotes the motto, "Don't be a writer; be writing." It's a good illustration that without doing the thing, the identity isn't real. Or, it may be that you are holding on to an old dream you should be letting go of, to make room for new dreams.

I'm not going to say it's easy to get unstuck when you've been stuck a long time. If it were easy, you would already have done it. The critical thing, I have found, is to focus on your own output rather than a hoped-for outcome. You don't go from graphic designer to movie star after one acting class. You don't get in Oprah's book club after writing one chapter. But you can take a class or write a chapter. And when you do, you will have accomplished that thing.

I've found there are two simple exercises to help when you've got something you really want to do but can't seem to ever get around to doing. These won't solve your problem, but they may help you figure out what your problem is.

1. **Define what success means to you**

   If you strip away all the things that are outside your control, how would you define success? For every Alan Rickman, there are a thousand Gary Goldstars. A regular person with a regular job who had talent, a dream, and a goal but who managed only a fraction of Rickman's achievements. Does that mean they all failed? Rickman never got an Oscar. Did he succeed or fail? The point is that there is no universal measure of success. So, define what would be good enough for you. What's the lowest bar for success? This is not your new target! Dream your dream and shoot for stardom. Why not? It can help, however, to articulate the lowest standard you would find acceptable if you never got any farther. Simply by articulating it—if you can define it and tell it to another person—you will figure out a lot about yourself and what, if anything, you should invest in pursuing the dream.

2. **Interview your future self**

   Every day you make decisions that mold your future self. Imagine traveling into the future to meet the person you've become in twenty years' time. This is a different person from who you are today. Interview that person about their life. Ask that person questions that get to meaning, values, and self-image unrelated to the dream you're currently wrestling with. You need to get your current self out of the way. Your current self is the one that's causing all the problems. Be curious about that other person who's waiting to meet you 20 years down the line. This kind of visualization exercise isn't for everyone, but if you can do it with an honest and open mind, you may see your life today from a very different perspective. Some questions you might ask your future self:

- What are you most proud of in the last 20 years?
- What do you wish you'd done differently over the last 20 years?
- Who were the most important people to you during that time?
- What do you want people to remember about you, or to remember you for?
- Who are the most important people to you today?

On the back of this page, write down your definitions of success. Start with what you really desire, if everything were to work out perfectly and you got everything you dream of. Next, write down the minimum you need to achieve in order to feel that all your time, effort, and energy weren't wasted. As long as your trajectory continues to be between those two, you're on the right track. If you drift outside that zone, it may be time to reevaluate your dream.

Describe what it's like if your wildest dreams come true.

Describe the absolute minimum you need to get in order to feel you haven't wasted your time, effort, or money.

Stop Planning and Take Action

Even the best plans and most sincere intentions amount to nothing if you never follow through. Some people seem to be always preparing for plans that never get done. It's like they're preparing for a vacation, but they keep re-packing the car and never actually leave the driveway. It's not just individuals (though that's what this book is about), but it happens with organizations, too.

I'm thinking of one particular company that's like that. They breathlessly announce an exciting, innovative strategic initiative or new direction, and they work hard to put everything in place for that new initiative. Then, just when they should leap into execution mode, everything grinds to a halt as they decide to reassess and return to strategizing.

I had a similar realization about myself at the last New Year's, as I was journaling to sort out my thoughts and brainstorm plans for the coming year. I realized that some of my brainstorming wasn't new. I was mostly coming up with ideas I'd already had. The fact that they were good ideas made little difference—I was falling into a cycle of thinking about my ideas instead of acting on them. A lot of people fall into this trap.

Once, at one of my workplaces some time ago, my boss complained to me about my predecessor in the job. He said, "The last guy spent all his time making lists of people to call, but he never actually called anyone. He just kept making new lists, re-filtering them, re-sorting them, and re-naming them." It was clear that my boss was not interested in me doing the same thing. And frankly, neither was I.

Objectively speaking, it's pretty obvious that I am a person who mostly acts on my ideas. In the past 12 months (as I write this chapter), I published two books, coached over 100 people, achieved my PCC coaching certification, moved from California to Oregon, and started two new workshop series. In fact, I'm more prone to act before I've fully defined my plan than I am to make a plan that goes undone… but it does happen sometimes. Like anyone, I can get stuck in a think-plan-rethink-replan circle that is hard to break out of.

But planning is not enough. Plans mean little if you never act on them. No one feels good when the answer to "why is this not done" is "well, I planned on doing that, but…" We all do it from time to time, of course. We are only human. If you catch yourself in a cycle of rethink-replan when you should have already moved on to execution, here are a few questions to ask yourself:

1. **Which isn't ready, the plan or you?**

   Something is keeping this from moving forward, so either the plan isn't solid enough to act on, or you are not ready to act on it. What do you need in order to be ready to move forward with this? Is there some knowledge you lack? A set of skills you don't have? Contacts you need? Insufficient funding? Identify the areas of need and fix them. Often, these require skills that aren't in your top strengths, so instead of fixing those areas, you fall into redoing the things that are easy and comfortable Many years ago, a friend and I had a great business plan and potential interest from venture capitalists. Unfortunately, although my friend was definitely ready to be a founder of a venture-backed company, I was not. I simply did not yet have the business experience, gravitas, presence, and confidence it would take, and we did not have a strong enough network to pull together a complete team. We decided against pursuing it. The plan had potential, but I was not ready to execute it.

2. **Do you believe in this plan?**

   It's possible you don't really believe in this plan. Perhaps it was concocted by others or handed to you by someone full of good advice. Or maybe it just has a flaw in it, or you simply aren't interested in doing it. What's holding you back from letting it go? I went through a period where I almost quit writing. I stopped believing in the publishing industry around 2010, when the internet had begun to change the publishing industry in fundamental and profound ways. I ended up abandoning my old plan of trying to get published, and I created a new plan to self-publish. Fifteen years later, I'm running my own imprint and teaching self-publishing workshops.

3. **What are you afraid of?**

   What about this plan makes you feel vulnerable or at risk? One of the hardest things in life is to discern whether that inner voice telling you to be careful is wisdom or fear. Fear is a strong anti-motivator, and it's often given too much power. What is truly at risk? Is your health, your livelihood, or something equally important truly at risk? If not, what are you afraid of? Say it out loud to a person you trust. Imagine the worst-case scenario and ask yourself whether you will have stronger regrets if that worst case comes to happen, or if you never take the leap in the first place. As I write this, I'm trying to think back to the times when I let fear hold me back. I can't remember those times. Not because it never happened—I am quite sure I've sabotaged myself by giving in to fear many times in my life—but because the memories I have are of the times I stepped out despite my fears. Looking back, the parts of my life I'm most proud of and remember most clearly are when I took risks. When I acted in spite of fear and vulnerability. Some of those times worked out. Some didn't. In all cases, the worst was never as bad as my fears had promised.

4. **What one step can you take *right now*?**

    The journey of 10,000 steps begins with one single step. You have to start somewhere; very few things leap out of your sketchbook fully formed in reality. What one step can you take *today*, no matter how small, to get started? Buy a domain name. Open a bank account. Register your LLC. Write "Chapter One" at the top of the page. Whatever you can do right now, do it. I started Gray Bear Coaching in early 2022 with a bunch of ideas, a lot of hope, and a mountain of unknowns. My plan was hardly what anyone would call fully formed. (Even today, it's pretty squishy.) But I started with a single blog post because it was a step I could take right then. I could never have gotten to 150 posts if I had not written the first one. I know a lot of people who still haven't taken that one first step, whatever it is. What happens afterward is never guaranteed, but you can't go anywhere if you keep repacking the car and never leave the driveway.

So take an action—any action—today. And yes, I mean *today*. Stop thinking about acting, and act. Stop re-packing the car, re-drawing the route, re-listing priorities, re-planning the plan. Do something. Take action.

Or don't. It's your life.

What one action will you take this month?

What one action will you take this week?

What one action will you take tomorrow?

If You Don't Fall Down, You're Not Having Enough Fun

One of the best pieces of advice I ever got was when I was nine years old and just learning to ski. My brother was 15 at the time and had been tasked with keeping me company on the slopes for part of the morning. I was timid and slow, snowplowing back and forth across the trail.

My brother was not what I would call a patient person. At least, as a 15-year-old, he did not demonstrate a saintly level of patience with his whiny nine-year-old brother, especially when said little brother was being a complete killjoy. He kept urging me to go faster. I kept whining that I was afraid that if I did, I would fall down. As long as I kept it slow and under control, I could stay upright. And wasn't that the goal, after all?

Then, as I lay in the snow, resting halfway down the slope, he pulled up next to me.

"If you don't fall down," he growled, "then you're not having enough fun."

Of course, we've all heard the old saw, if you don't fall down, then you're not trying hard enough. I like my brother's version better. The idea that you should keep working harder and harder until you injure yourself seems pretty cynical. But I can get behind the idea of pushing the envelope in pursuit of joy.

I frequently think of that whenever I find myself retreating into a cautious mindset.

If you are looking for a fulfilling life, you might need to take risks from time to time in pursuit of that fulfillment.

If you don't fall down, you're not having enough fun.

How is fear of falling down (embarrassment, failure, loss, etc.) keeping you from taking a risk you want to take?

What Gets Measured Gets Managed

It's an incredibly simple concept, but it's shocking how often we forget this: what you give attention to will thrive, and what you starve for attention will wither.

If you have several plants in your garden and you spend all your energy and time tending only half of them, those plants will thrive while the neglected ones will not. (This is a bad metaphor in my case; gardening skipped a generation in my family. All the plants will die if I am the one tasked with tending them.)

This holds true no matter what kind of metaphorical garden you're talking about: Your professional network. Personal pet projects. Healthy living habits. Job skills. Personal relationships.

It's important to find ways to measure where you spend your time and attention. Because what gets measured, gets managed. The things you track end up getting more of your attention.

Humans are terrible self-reporters. We judge ourselves and our situation on feelings rather than on actual data. We believe we understand truth because we are living it, but in reality those feelings are filtered through all our biases, first-person perspective, fears, and desires. Since we don't measure things in our daily lives, those feelings become self-fulfilling truths. Confirmation bias makes us highlight evidence that supports those feelings while ignoring evidence that refutes them. We become invested in those feelings and even start defending them.

This is how two spouses can each think they're doing more than half the household chores. That's obviously not possible unless they're duplicating effort, which is a different problem. Over time, unless the couple measure who does what when, each will begin resenting the other. Arguments will erupt over tiny things, each person convinced they are doing more than the other and each convinced the other is refusing to see the truth. They'll bring their own evidence to the fight and downplay evidence presented against them.

Yes, I speak from experience (though not household chores), and I've also seen this play out in workplaces, in families, and even with internal dialog. I can't tell you how many clients have told me they feel a certain way, and then paint a picture of the exact opposite, all the while continuing to believe the feelings over the evidence they're presenting. This usually shows up as self-doubt (in the case of a successful person feeling not successful enough) or resentment at others (in the case of not getting recognized for what they think they should be recognized for).

My first memory of this phenomenon was when I was in startups in the 1990s. One of the engineers left the startup where I was working and went to another company, one that was in a growth phase after going public. He told me not long after the switch that the job was so easy it was almost boring. He said, "Everyone at this new company thinks they're working really hard, but I'd say they're putting in half the effort I'm used to. They have no idea what hard work is."

My most recent memory of this was several years ago. I was working for an extremely busy manager with a very narrow idea of what my job entailed. He only understood about 30% of what I had to do every day. After a while, he began hinting that perhaps I wasn't working very hard. It was one of those "I don't know what you do all day, so you must not be doing anything of value" situations. I understood my job and knew I was working very hard, so I ignored his veiled hints… until I got a surprisingly bad performance review, even though my high-level outcomes were all satisfactory or better.

At the time, I thought it was unfair, but I had no recourse. He had built up an unfounded belief that I was not performing well, and I had nothing but my own belief to counter it with. Today, years later, I am completely certain his assessment was unfair. That's partly due to perspective and distance, but it's mostly due to what I did next. I started to track my activities. I did not want to get caught in an unfair performance review again without data to counter that false narrative.

Here's what I did: Every day after arriving at the office, I opened my "activity log" document and put today's date at the top. This was just simple text document where I wrote down everything I did throughout the day. Everything from "approved the social media tile for next week's event" to "met with Charlie about his conflict with George."

It was nothing fancy, just a log of my activities. Not my *accomplishments*—my *activities*. The things I spent my time on. Because that was what my boss couldn't see. He saw the end results—the *accomplishments*—but thought I could be doing so much more because he significantly underestimated the work that went into achieving most of them, and he completely undervalued others.

I kept at this for a few months as a daily practice. It became a habit. Many years later, I still do this and have found it incredibly useful as an entrepreneur in charge of my own schedule, activities, and outputs.

Through this process, I learned two truly valuable things:

1. I was actually doing a lot more than I had been giving myself credit for, and
2. On days when I was underperforming (we all have days like that), by lunchtime I would see the list was way too short, and it would light a fire under me to get more done in the afternoon.

I have kept this daily practice and improved it over the years to fit my workstyle. I've added naming conventions, some color coding, prioritization, and other nuances that work for me. It's not a tool I can package and sell because it's simply a word processing document. I'm not a fan of over-engineering a process, and the one ehat's best is the one you actually do.

As you move forward with the things you're going to do to create your fulfilling life, make sure you're measuring the important things. Keep track of what truly matters to you and your process because what gets measured gets managed. If you're measuring the wrong thing, you may end up with the wrong results. If you're not measuring at all, you may be making decisions based on fear, assumption, bias, or magical thinking.

Measuring is what gets you off the fince to make good decisions.

What are some of the everyday tools you use to keep track of your priority to-dos, your activities, and your achievements?

In what area(s) of your life would having clearer statistics allow you to improve your own effectiveness?

How can you use those existing tools to begin rudimentary measurement of the important statistics in those areas?

Celebrate Success

We spend a lot of our time comparing ourselves to others, or comparing where we are to where we want to be. From time to time, it's important to compare where you are to how far you've come.

Most of us, especially the high achievers that have gotten this far in this book, tend to finish a thing and then immediately think about the next thing that needs doing. We move the goal posts on ourselves. The current situation becomes our new baseline, replacing the previous baseline. This serves to keep you moving forward, but it can also be exhausting.

Take a moment to think back over the last six months. How far have you come? Take your time with this question. This question is not an opportunity to beat yourself up, but you probably will anyway. I've noticed that when people answer quickly, they list the two or three big accomplishments that leap to mind, and then they immediately pivot to all the things they meant to do but didn't, or the next things on their list.

When people take their time with this question, though, I've found they are often surprised at how much they end up congratulating themselves for. This is true even for people who can legitimately say they had a dreadful six months. There's often a lot more in the "done" column than high achievers recognize at first. I think this is because we don't have clear "before" and "after" pictures to look at, like those home renovation shows on television. Bear with me:

The typical home renovation show has a *before*, a *brief*, and an *after*. It goes like this:

- They show us the existing home. This is the *before*.
- The client describes everything they dream of for their redesigned home. This is the *brief*.
- The host gets a bid from the contractor that is waaaaay outside the budget. To stay within budget, the client has to scale back their expectations. After the work begins, the contractor finds hidden problems that make some of the renovations impossible and increase the cost of others.
- Finally, the Big Reveal happens, and the client is thrilled with the result. This is the *after*.

There may be some discussion during the Big Reveal about the compromises and omissions, but in every show that I've ever seen, the client ends up beyond happy even though the end product has fallen far short of the original dreamed-of result.

"That's not real life," you may be saying. "That's television. Of course the clients are happy. They're on TV. They're probably under contract to pretend to be happy."

My inner cynic wants to agree with you, but I think the clients' happiness is genuine. Why? Because they're not comparing the end result to the dream; they're comparing the end result to the original.

The client gets a dose of reality early in the process, resetting their expectations. Then the producers of the show are smart enough to keep showing us the *before* photos all along the way. What was ugly? What was broken? What were the problems? They also show us the work in progress. Things torn apart. Chaos and indecision. Difficult choices.

Then, in the Big Reveal, they show the client the final result of all that work and investment. All we see at that point are the improvements. We see the clever solutions, the interesting design, the beautiful handiwork. They don't show us the things that didn't happen. The things that were left undone aren't highlighted. The hosts only talk about compromises made if the end result is clever and worth celebrating.

In this way, they have us comparing the work that was done to the original starting point. We're comparing the *after* to the *before*, rather than comparing the *after* to the *brief*. High achievers do the opposite of this when we judge our own performance. We focus on the things left undone, the mistakes made, and the compromises allowed. We do this so much, we may not even consider ourselves "high achievers" because we ignore what we do accomplish.

Although I hear this with many of my clients, I remember one particular client from a few years ago who was extreme about ignoring her successes and highlighting her failures and omissions. She would tell me about all the things she'd accomplished in the prior few weeks, then immediately pivot to how she should have done them sooner, how she didn't do them as well as she wanted, and how there were so many other things left undone.

It was in working with her that I first used this analogy of the renovation show's brief/before/after approach. Over the next several sessions as we worked together, I heard her language change and saw her confidence increase, as she paid more attention to acknowledging her accomplishments. She successfully moved herself out of a constant feeling of failure and inadequacy by realizing and changing three things that high achievers are prone to doing:

- We constantly compare our current situation to the ultimate goal (the *brief*) instead of to where we started (the *before*). Make sure to look back periodically to appreciate how far you've come from your starting point.
- Every time we hit a milestone, we reset our idea of the starting point (the *before*) to this new position. When you're considering your own growth and progress, don't just look back to the most recent milestone. Look all the way back to the beginning, and count how many milestones you passed along the way.
- Every time we reach a goal, we move the goalposts. By reimagining and rewriting the *brief* every time we make any

progress, we constantly compare where we are to a more difficult ideal.

You may be arguing that these three things are how progress happens. And you're right! To move forward after achieving a goal, you have to set a new goal and keep striving toward it. These habits are also exhausting. If you've ever felt like you're on a hamster wheel, this may be why. It's critical for your own pacing and mental health to pause and give yourself (and others!) credit for how far you've come. Stop achieving for thirty minutes. Really stop. Look back at the path you've traveled, the things you've done. Don't stop contemplating after remembering just two or three big accomplishments. Take in the full view of your recent history. Admire the details. List out all the things you actually did during that time. Not just positive accomplishments toward your goal, but everything that you did and the crises you had to respond to. Because that's what life is. It's full of compromises, accidents, and unavoidable situations not of your own making. And, it's full of accomplishments.

Have you ever noticed that on TV, home renovation projects never actually fail? They may, but I've never seen it. Admittedly, I don't watch a lot of home improvement shows these days. In the real world, home renovation projects fail all the time. Feuds erupt between contractors and subcontractors. Miscommunications and misunderstandings undermine progress. Deals fall through. Marriages fall apart.

So, what's the difference between the real world and the TV world? The TV world has producers and editors who keep everyone's focus on what makes for enjoyable TV: There is tension along the way, but in the end everyone must be happy with the outcome. They set the talent up for success by ensuring that the storyline is about how much better the end product (the *after*) is than where they started (the *before*). They spend hardly any time at all contemplating how much was left undone or how many corners had to be cut along the way.

This isn't deception. It's simply managing perspective. Staying focused on the positive. There's always positive to be celebrated. Unfortunately, in life and business we don't have editors and producers carefully curating our storyline and ensuring the story's focus stays positive. That's work you need to do yourself as you move forward. Because if you're constantly resetting your expectations and moving your own goalposts, you'll find that you can never *have* a fulfilling life because you are always *pursuing* a fulfilling life.

If you're always chasing happiness, you will never be in happiness.

Write down several things you're proud of from the past year. Use extra paper. The space below isn't hardly big enough.

Section 4

Conclusion

Every New Year's, I think about my aspirations for the coming year. Many of us do this. Then, at the end of the year, we look back to see how many of those aspirations turned into accomplishments. Last New Year's, several of my 2024 aspirations had been left undone. And I think that's wonderful.

Don't get me wrong. I know from my activity log that I accomplished an amazing amount of truly impressive stuff in 2024. From publishing TWIST and RELIT, to running several workshops, to leveling up my coaching credential, to moving myself and my business from California to Oregon, to many other accomplishments. By any measure, it was a productive and fulfilling year.

If I had achieved every aspiration on my list, however, then maybe I dreamed too small. That's why I like to have at least some aspirations left undone every year.

This may be one reason I rarely feel disappointed in my own performance. Disappointment has no place in a system where *left undone* is not considered failure. *Left undone* is simply a fact, with no morality or judgment attached. There may be consequences to face, but my character and value as a person are not in question.

I am just trying to make the most of every day because I don't know when I passed the halfway point of my life. At 57 years old, it's likely that the second half of my life started some time ago. I have no idea how many days I have left. I'd like to make the most of each one of them. That leaves me little time for regret and unreasonable self-judgment.

I did not come to this mindset by accident or in a single weekend retreat. It has been the work of years, and it is ongoing.

I understand my core values. I put myself in position to use my strengths as much as possible. I set my goals high. I track where I spend my time. I remember to look back and celebrate not just my successes but also how far I've come. I take risks because if I don't fall down, then I'm not having enough fun. I show up, I try hard, and I try to be nice. I check in periodically with my future self and forgive my past self. I keep learning and asking new questions. I get outside perspectives. And I measure what matters.

I hope when my second half ends, I will depart with no regrets and several things left undone. That will mean that I dreamed big, tried hard, stayed true to myself, and made the most of this life, one day at a time.

Acknowledgements

I'd like to say this book was written in a year, but that year wasn't possible without three years of coaching hundreds of people, 30 years of managing teams and working with amazing colleagues, a diverse group of wise and fun-loving friends, a number of outstanding teachers, and of course my parents, my brother, my sister, and my own awesome children. I am also grateful to the many people who helped me become the writer I am and the many clients who put their trust in me to help them find their path in life. And I am profoundly grateful to my partner, Antoinette, who coaches me as much as I coach her.

Where to Learn More

There are over 150 articles on life, leadership, courage, fulfillment, and other important topics at the graybearcoaching.com blog as well as several exercises including core values and life purpose assessments.

Peter is available for one-on-one executive and life coaching, team facilitation, and workshops on fulfillment, courageous living, overcoming burnout and compassion fatigue, communicating powerfully, and leading with empathy and wisdom. Go to graybearcoaching.com to schedule a free, no-obligation conversation.

Want to tell your story or get your book published? Gray Bear Publications can help. Visit graybearpublications.com to learn about our book coaching, assisted self-publishing services, and current calls for submissions.

 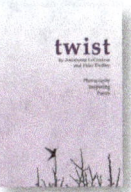 

More from the Author at peterdudley.com

Peter has published multiple books, including:

- ***RELIT: How to Rekindle Yourself in the Darkness of Compassion Fatigue***
  This multi-author book offers practical, relevant advice and inspiring stories from a variety of experts.
- ***Semper*, *Forsada*, and *Freda*: The New Eden trilogy**
  A post-apocalyptic young adult trilogy about the intersection of truth, faith, and prejudice.
- ***Together* and *Twist***
  Two collections of poetry and photography co-authored with Antoinette LeCouteur.
- ***Lifelike***
  A contemporary urban fantasy about a young woman finding her courage.

About the Author
Peter J Dudley, PCC

Peter is an award-winning author and executive coach who helps people find their courage to live and lead with authenticity and clarity. He grew up in Connecticut with summers in Las Vegas, got his electrical engineering degree from UC Berkeley, then went on a 30-year career in startups, nonprofits, and big corporations with a focus on social impact, employee engagement, and innovation. Peter has published four novels, two poetry collections, and a chapter book, and his short fiction and professional articles have been published in a variety of journals and anthologies. He is also the editor and publisher of RELIT: *How to Rekindle Yourself in the Darkness of Compassion Fatigue.* Find him at graybearcoaching.com.

www.ingramcontent.com/pod-product-compliance
Lightning Source LLC
LaVergne TN
LVHW020430070526
838199LV00025B/584/J